Let's *"not forget to do good and to share with others, for with such sacrifices God is pleased"* (Hebrews 13:16).

A STRATEGY FOR
MEETING NEEDS IN
YOUR COMMUNITY

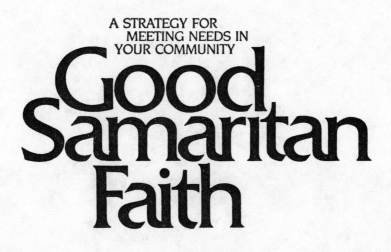

Good Samaritan Faith

BERNARD THOMPSON

A Division of GL Publications
Ventura, CA U.S.A.

Scripture quotations in this publication, unless otherwise indicated. arc from the *New International Version*, Holy Bible. Copyright © 1973 and 1978 by New York International Bible Society. Used by permission. Also quoted is *NEB, The New English Bible.* © The Delegates of the Oxford University Press and The Syndics of the Cambridge University Press 1961, 1970. Reprinted by permission.

© 1984 by Bernard Thompson
All rights reserved

Published by Regal Books
A Division of GL Publications
Ventura, California 93006
Printed in U.S.A.

Library of Congress Cataloging in Publication Data

Thompson, Bernard, 1949-
    Good Samaritan faith.

    Bibliography: p.
    1. Lay ministry. 2. Church and social problems.
I. Title.
BV4400.T47   1984   253   83-24805
ISBN 0-8307-0932-0

To
Cheryl,
Matthew,
Andrew,
and
Jonathan.

CONTENTS

Acknowledgments

I could not have written *Good Samaritan Faith* without the constant encouragement and support of my family. I've dedicated this book to Cheryl, Matthew, Andrew, and Jonathan to express my thanks to them, and because we want to dedicate ourselves, as a family, to keep on learning how we can have a caring life-style.

My good friend, Dan Rich (a publishing and marketing consultant) first suggested I should write this book. Dan's encouragement has been a rich source of inspiration, practical help, and wise guidance—throughout many creative projects I've had the privilege of working on with him.

Many other friends have helped with their prayers, personal support, and friendship.

While most of the book is based on actual ministry experience, I've also drawn freely on the helpful writings of various visionary, compassionate, author/teachers—including John Stott, Ronald J. Sider, Tom Sine, and Donald Kraybill. They are just a few of those whose writings continue to challenge and guide my attempts to learn more about how to live out the Christian faith in a needy world.

I'm especially grateful to the staff of the Vernon

Grounds Center for Learning at the Conservative Baptist Seminary in Denver, Colorado, for allowing me to use their library. Dr. Ronald Bard, executive director of Evangelical Concern of Denver, also graciously gave me some of his precious time for a helpful personal interview.

My thanks to the pastoral staff, lay leaders, and members of Pulpit Rock Church in Colorado Springs, who've all provided lots of opportunities to discuss, study, and test many of the approaches and ideas described in this book. My friends and co-volunteers in Northern Churches Care in Colorado Springs have also modeled how Christians from different denominations can work together effectively and harmoniously. Although many different people have influenced my ideas about how to start a caring ministry in a local church, I accept final responsibility for the views expressed in *Good Samaritan Faith*.

May this book stimulate many Christians to launch local church-based caring ministries dedicated to serving people and glorifying God.

Preface

Good Samaritan Faith explains how a lay person can start a ministry of social concern in a local church. It is a book for concerned Christians who want to do something about meeting physical and social needs— as well as spiritual and personal needs—in Jesus' name.

Individual Christians and local churches *can* do something about many basic human needs and problems such as unemployment, hunger, lack of shelter, and poverty which increasingly affect people everywhere. *Good Samaritan Faith* focuses on simple suggestions and projects which can be carried out by individuals, small groups, and local churches. And it introduces the reader to some books that provide more detailed discussions of Christian social concern and action.

But before local churches can care—either for their own members or for others outside their church—the individual Christians within those churches must learn how to care.

> The future of the world is in the hands of those who care, not on a limited scale—myself, my

family, my class, my race, my party—but in the hands of those who care with unlimited caring.

Those words, written in 1968 by E. Stanley Jones in *A Song of Ascents,* are still true today.

If *Good Samaritan Faith* encourages the reader to grow in the grace of unlimited caring—loving others in a variety of practical ways for Jesus' sake—it will accomplish its purpose.

Introduction

"What would it take to start a new church?" I often asked myself a few years ago.

I dreamed of a local church that would help every member feel he or she belonged to a caring community. A church in which all areas of one's life were valued. A church which surrounded all members with the love of Christ.

I dreamed of a local church which freed each person to use all of his or her God-given gifts. A church which encouraged everyone to reach his or her full spiritual maturity in Christ. This caring local church would also care about the surrounding community.

The church members would have God's mission on their hearts. They would get to know their neighbors, and share their love for God through attractive, Christ-centered, genuinely caring life-styles. They would keep each other informed about local, national, and international affairs. They would understand the challenge of the church's global mission in today's world. This church's vision would balance a concern for its own with a desire to bring the good news to people everywhere. The teaching ministry would balance an emphasis on each member's spiritual growth with a biblically-based emphasis on ministry to the whole person. A willingness to meet physical and social needs would be included in the church's ministry objectives.

The members of this local church would display a shared commitment to the Lord, His Word, His world, and to one another. They would be actively reaching out with God's love. They would demonstrate the reality of their faith by living out the whole gospel, by caring for one another, and by doing something about hunger, poverty, moral issues, and questions of justice in contemporary life. I dreamed about such a committed, caring local church and wanted to help fulfill its vision. I dreamed of a local church whose members would learn how to "think globally and act locally."

The more I prayed and thought about my dream church, the less interested I became in starting another actual church. My wife, Cheryl, and I had been attending our local church for several years. We grew through our pastors' faithful expositions of God's Word. But we couldn't shake a feeling of being just a little too comfortable. At the same time, we met three other couples (all from another church in our city) who shared our concerns. We all wanted to make our faith count in the real world. We did not want to avoid studying the so-called "hard" passages of the gospel. We hungered for a discipleship that would do something about tough issues like poverty and hunger.

Another friend traveled widely among Christian fellowships in the developing nations. As we listened to his reports, we heard about believers in other countries who wondered whether Western Christians like us really cared about our brothers and sisters in the world's materially poorer countries. We cared, and we determined to do something, so we began meeting weekly to share, pray, and encourage each other.

As we searched the Scriptures, prayed, and discussed our insights, we sensed that the Lord wanted us to live out our faith at home—in our families, neighborhoods, offices, schools, and within our local churches.

After a few months we stopped meeting regularly because one couple was leaving for seminary. However, our small group had accomplished its purpose: Each of us had a clearer picture of what we thought the Lord wanted us to do as individuals and as couples.

Cheryl and I soon joined an adult Sunday School class at our local church. We offered to help the pastor, who was teaching the class, in any way we could. We took part in some panel discussions, enjoyed his class, and got to know some other members of our church who also wanted to study the biblical basis for Christian social concern.

One evening, the pastor we had helped called. He explained he was putting together the next quarter's adult electives. He asked me if I would be interested in teaching. Immediately, as we talked over the phone, he and I worked out an outline for a one-quarter class. Since I was leaving town for a week the next morning, and as he needed to get a class description printed right away, that was all the time we had. We called the class, "Christian Life-style in a Changing World." A few weeks later I had thirty eager adults in my class. At the end of the quarter many of them wanted to form an action group of some sort. They wanted to keep studying related topics, and several wanted to do some projects in our church and community.

My dream was becoming a reality! A caring ministry was forming in the midst of our local church. I didn't need to start another church just to see my dream fulfilled. Our small group's prayers were being answered! The class became an ongoing caring/action ministry known as the Barnabas Group. As well as doing some local church-based caring projects as a group, some of the class members became more involved in already-existing local church ministries, while others have become leaders in community-based action groups and ministries.

While teaching the Christian life-style class and forming the Barnabas Group, we used many of the excellent books dealing with hunger, Christian social responsibility, poverty, injustice, and world missions today. Many of them provide an excellent biblical overview of such topics, but at the time the class began I did not know of any books which practically described how a lay person can begin a ministry of social concern in a local church.

So I have written *Good Samaritan Faith* to provide a practical resource for the lay person who wants to do just that. I am a layman, and I have written this book for lay men and women. *Good Samaritan Faith* gives the lay person a practical guide on how to start a local church-based caring ministry. Throughout, I've suggested biblical and practical principles which will help. I've also emphasized the importance of integrating such a ministry with all of the other ministries of the local church, and suggested practical guidelines you can adapt. The book encourages you to minister in your neighborhood, community, nation, and world. It also encourages Christians to work cooperatively in ministries of social concern, and examines the relevance of simpler life-styles for more effective outreach and service.

You can use this book as a personal study guide or as a resource for small group discussions. Study the biblical guidelines for caring and sharing for yourself. Develop your own convictions about the local church's responsibility to its members and the local community. Develop your own vision for your local church by learning to "think globally and act locally."

Your church may be waiting for you to pray, dream, plan, and start just such a ministry. Look to the Lord for guidance. Share your dream with a few like-minded men and women. Explain your ministry goals to your pastor and other church leaders. Ask for their counsel and act upon their advice. Go to work wholeheartedly!

Launch a caring/action ministry in your church!

As you read, pray, and act, keep the example of your Lord constantly in mind. His life and ministry will continuously inspire and guide you as you follow His timeless example. For, as Peter once said, "You know about Jesus of Nazareth, how God anointed him with the Holy Spirit and with power. He went about doing good and healing all who were oppressed by the devil, for God was with him" (Acts 10:38, *NEB*).

May God be with you as you follow Jesus of Nazareth and serve Him in your local church, in your community, and wherever else He leads you to serve His people in His world.

Chapter 1

The Need for Caring Ministries

As I was writing this book, my unpredictable free-lance writer's income began drying up—slowly but surely. When my last major monthly client called to say his organization was cancelling all free-lance work for "economic reasons," I began to discover how it feels when you can't pay the bills. I worried about making house payments. I felt a parent's anguish as I struggled to provide food for my children.

But all during this stressful time Cheryl and I experienced the Lord's faithfulness. Sometimes we wondered if God heard our prayers, but other times He clearly demonstrated His concern for us through His people—our family, Christian friends, and our local church. Once my in-laws helped us make an overdue house payment. Another month two families gave us groceries, and the next month another couple gave us a check designated for food. Throughout those difficult months we never missed any meals. God supplied our needs. Although this experience hardly compares with what most of the world's desperately poor people face every day, it taught us much and helped us to identify more closely with the poor.

Like many others who have experienced sudden unemployment, our family learned to make do or do without. We were stretched emotionally and spiritually. We began to learn how to let others minister to us. And we learned something about endurance.

During this time I did everything possible to find work. I contacted more than thirty companies and organizations that employ writers or editors. Although I turned up a couple of projects, nothing came along that would meet my family's needs on a long-term basis. After several discouraging conversations with potential employers I felt first-hand the frustrations of being unemployed. I also rediscovered the importance of having close friends who would listen patiently to my struggles and pray regularly for me and my family.

When we began thinking about selling our home and moving to find work, my last interviewer called me back for a second interview. Four days later I accepted a copywriting job in the marketing department of a legal publishing company. Then we knew the joy of answered prayer. We resolved to remember the lessons we learned and to make ourselves available to minister to people with similar needs. This experience taught us something we couldn't have learned any other way.

Previously, I'd only read about poverty or observed the poor while living and traveling in several Asian countries and when visiting some of the larger cities in North America. Now, at least to some degree, I've felt what it's like to be poor.

My experience is quite common in today's world. In the 1980s a worldwide recession introduced hundreds of thousands of previously comfortable individuals to the cold reality of unemployment and the inability to provide adequately for themselves and their families.

As a result, Christians everywhere have become more aware than ever before of the personal dimensions of poverty. Once poverty seemed confined to people who lived on the wrong side of the tracks or the other side of the world. Not anymore. Every Christian today knows someone who is out of work, underemployed, or struggling to survive. Once poverty was the face of a starving child in a magazine or fund-raising letter. But today poverty may be seen in the face of my relative, my neighbor, and my fellow believer at church.

Even in comparatively rich, high-tech societies like the United States, sudden changes in the global and national economy have created large groups of new poor. Alert Christians who are in touch with the times recognize the need to forge new caring strategies to minister to this ever-growing group. As this happens, individual Christians and churches are also learning to care about ministering to the traditional poor—the desperately poor who have often been neglected by the church. Local churches are mobilizing individuals and small groups today to care for both the old poor and the new poor.

If you have a friend who is unemployed, or know a family in need, then you have seen the face of poverty. As an individual Christian, you can do something to minister to your needy brother or sister. And you can join with other Christians in your local church who want to work together to battle against the causes of poverty in your city, town, or neighborhood. *You* can make a difference in our needy world.

A Biblical Response to Human Need

The contemporary explosion of human need may present the church in North America with its greatest opportunity to make a lasting ministry impact on this continent. But this will only happen if individual Christians and local churches act.

Act we must, for the Lord we serve watches over His people. He watches us closely, as we learn in Isaiah 58, to see whether our religious commitments translate into practical acts of service to the hungry and homeless in our midst.

Is not this the kind of fasting I have chosen:
to loose the chains of injustice
  and untie the cords of the yoke.
to set the oppressed free
  and break every yoke?
Is it not to share your food with the hungry
  and to provide the poor wanderer with
  shelter—
when you see the naked, to clothe him,
  and not to turn away from your own flesh and
  blood?
Then your light will break forth like the dawn,
  and your healing will quickly appear;
then your righteousness will go before you,
  and the glory of the Lord will be your rear
  guard.
Then you will call, and the Lord will answer;
  you will cry for help, and he will say: Here am
  I.
If you do away with the yoke of oppression,
  with the pointing finger and malicious talk,
and if you spend yourselves on behalf of the
  hungry
  and satisfy the needs of the oppressed,
then your light will rise in the darkness,
  and your night will become like the noonday.
The Lord will guide you always;
  he will satisfy your needs in a sun-scorched
  land
  and will strengthen your frame.
You will be like a well-watered garden,
  like a spring whose waters never fail.
Your people will rebuild the ancient ruins
  and will raise up the age-old foundations;
you will be called Repairer of Broken Walls,
  Restorer of Streets with Dwellings

(Isa. 58:6-12).

Jesus also clearly stated what He expects from each of His followers. In Matthew 25 He tells His disciples that He identifies personally with the hungry, homeless, sick, and imprisoned. At the judgment, those who faithfully apply the biblical teachings on caring for the needy will hear their King say,

"Come, you who are blessed by my Father; take your inheritance, the kingdom prepared for you since the creation of the world. For I was hungry and you gave me something to eat, I was thirsty and you gave me something to drink, I was a stranger, and you invited me in, I needed clothes and you clothed me, I was sick and you looked after me, I was in prison and you came to visit me . . . . Whatever you did for one of the least of these brothers of mine, you did for me" (Matt. 25:34-36,40).

On another occasion Jesus was approached by a lawyer who asked, "Teacher, what must I do to inherit eternal life?" (Luke 10:25).

Jesus asked the lawyer if he knew the Old Testament answer to that question. Although he replied correctly, "'Love the Lord your God with all your heart and with all your soul and with all your strength and with all your mind'; and, 'Love your neighbor as yourself'" (Luke 10:27), the lawyer had another question for Jesus: "Who is my neighbor?" (10:29).

In reply Jesus said: "A man was going down from Jerusalem to Jericho, when he fell into the hands of robbers. They stripped him of his clothes, beat him and went away, leaving him half dead. A priest happened to be going down the same road, and when he saw the man, he passed by on the other side. So too, a Levite, when he came to the place and saw him, passed by on the other side. But a Samaritan, as he traveled, came where the man was; and when he saw him, he took pity on him. He went to him and bandaged his wounds, pouring on oil and wine. Then he put the man on his own donkey, took him to an inn and took care of him. The next day he took out two silver coins and gave them to the innkeeper. 'Look after him,' he said, 'and when I return, I will reimburse you for any extra expense you may have.' Which of these three do you think was a neighbor to the man who fell into the hands of robbers?" The expert in the law replied, "The one who had mercy on him." Jesus told him, "Go and do likewise" (Luke 10:30-37).

The Good Samaritan saw someone in need, and responded with faith, love, and action. He gave the wounded man first-aid, and helped him regain his health and strength by taking him to an inn where he paid the innkeeper to look after the wounded stranger. The Good Samaritan also returned later to check up on the stranger's recovery.

With this simple illustration, Jesus defined neighbor love and challenged the lawyer to "Go and do likewise" (Luke 10:37). Jesus' challenge remains the same for us today. "Good Samaritan Faith" identifies a need then takes practical action to meet that need.

The Good Samaritan did not have to get involved when he saw the wounded man. He *chose* to get involved and took action in a potentially dangerous situation. In doing so, he demonstrated how to personally obey the second greatest commandment.

Scriptures like these compel us to act in loving service to help needy people. All Christians must deliberately resist the temptation to spiritualize such texts. Instead, we must read them carefully and then apply the plain meaning of the words of God to the human needs we see in our neighborhoods and local communities. We must hear again Jesus' command to teach others everything He taught the Twelve (Matt. 28:20). He modeled a personal ministry of compassionate service, as well as a public preaching ministry. His life combined "doing good and healing" (Acts 10:38) with announcing the coming of God's Kingdom. Do we follow His example, or do we need to reexamine our commitment and willingness to meet practical and physical needs?

The biblical evidence is quite plain if we are willing to study the whole Bible and apply the whole text to our individual and corporate lives. We only need to study the Word honestly, openly, and obediently to begin discerning how God would have us minister to others. Many scholars have already laid the groundwork in their studies of social themes in the Bible.

Orlando Costas, a professor of missiology at Eastern Baptist Theological Seminary in Philadelphia, Pennsylvania, helpfully explains the biblical teachings which refer to the poor in both the Old and New Testaments in *The Integrity of Mission:*

> Although in the Old Testament tradition, the *poor* came to signify both the pious of the Lord (that is, those who opened themselves to the Lord and waited upon him) as well as those who were deprived of the basic essentials of life, *overwhelming attention is concentrated on the latter* [italics added]. For example, of approximately 235 references in the Old Testament where the five leading terms for the poor may be found *(ebyon, dal, ani, anaw, rash)*, only twenty-five can be identified with "poverty of spirit," or "meekness." Thus the poor are referred to sixty-one times as "beggars" *(ebyon)*; forty-eight times as "bent-over-ones" *(ani)*; twenty-five times as "indigent or needy" *(rash)*.

That emphasis seems to be retained in the New Testament, at least with the most frequently used term, *ptochos*, which means the "wretched ones." This word appears thirty-four times and only on six occasions does it refer to "spiritual poverty."

This quantitative evidence shows *at least* that the Bible takes seriously those who are materially poor. Those who are socially, economically and politically marginated, who are powerless because they are deprived of the basic essentials of life; are said to have God on their side. Their condition is a scandal and an insult to God who created humankind in his image, to live in community and look after one another.[1]

The Bible teaches that practical social action to relieve human need ought to be the partner of our evangelistic concern. As the Apostle John writes, "If anyone has material possessions and sees his brother in need but has no pity on him, how can the love of God be in him? Dear children, let us not love with words or tongue but with actions and in truth" (1 John 3:17-18).

Commenting on this key passage, John Stott notes how love in action springs from seeing a brother in need and having the resources to meet that need. Stott adds:

If I do not relate what I "have" to what I "see," I cannot claim to be indwelt by the love of God. Further, this principle applies whatever the nature of the seen need. I may see spiritual need (sin, guilt, lostness) and have the gospel knowledge to meet it. Or the need I see may be disease or ignorance or bad housing, and I may have the medical, educational or social expertise to relieve it. To see need and to possess the remedy compels love to act, and whether the action will be evangelistic or social, or indeed political, depends on what we "see" and what we "have."[2]

Personal Bible study is one effective way to learn about how to see need and act compassionately in response to need. This was demonstrated in the results of a *Christianity Today* survey which found that regular Bible readers consider helping the poor personally an inescapable responsibility. According to the survey, frequent Bible readers are more likely than others to actually do something for the poor in their own community.[3]

Careful personal Bible study, therefore, provides an essential foundation for obeying our Lord's commands to care for others in practical ways. But as well as reading and rereading our Bibles, we also need to learn how to read the times in which we live. We must study the signs of our times as well as our Bibles. We must learn what social trends, economic changes, educational influences, and political events are currently shaping our world. The more familiar we are with our world—locally, nationally, and internationally—the more effective we will become in communicating our timeless message in a way that meets the real needs of our neighbors, work mates, and friends. We must learn how to make friends in the non-Christian community. We must learn how to demonstrate a faith that works in the marketplace. For a faith revealed only in the sanctuary cannot be seen by non-believers who never visit our churches. So we must study our world, and humbly live out our faith in the midst of present-day human need.

The Challenge to Local Churches

We do not need to travel overseas to observe the widening gap between rich and poor. The rich are getting richer and the poor are getting poorer on our own doorsteps.

Everywhere there is an explosion of social need.

Soup kitchens, emergency housing shelters, food pantries, and welfare agencies from coast to coast are overwhelmed by the numbers seeking assistance. Caseworkers and volunteers are overworked, and the need for donations of food, clothing, medical aid, and money, as well as volunteer counseling services, has never been greater. Social workers and church volunteers alike worry about how they will cope with this seemingly endless demand—especially during the winter months of each year.

American Christians are becoming increasingly aware of the need for new caring ministries as they observe the effects of these trends within their own congregations. While poverty may be studied at the national level, it is felt on the local level in one's own home, work place, and community. In response, churches in many cities across the country are organizing social ministries and cooperating with other churches and social agencies to provide financial aid, food, and spiritual counsel to the unemployed.

Some families are fighting for survival just around the corner from your local church. Do your church members simply drive by on their way to Sunday services, or are you actively caring for hurting families in your church's neighborhood?

We must wake up our brothers and sisters in Christ. We must pray that God will give us the eyes to see human need and the courage to respond in faith and love. How will we respond to the contemporary explosion of need? Each church, each Christian family, each Christian person must answer this question according to local needs and opportunities.

An issue like unemployment must surely motivate us to share our resources with the members of our churches who are out of work. Clearly, this is a biblical responsibility: "Therefore, as we have opportunity, let us do good to all people, especially to those who belong to the family of believers" (Gal. 6:10). Every local church needs at least some basic emergency network that is able to provide counseling, food, and/or financial aid to members with valid needs.

As we begin to respond to the needs of our brothers and sisters in Christ, we will become increasingly aware of similar needs among the unchurched. Caring can then be integrated with our evangelistic outreach. Church members can organize food collections and take food to needy families who live near their churches and in their members' neighborhoods. As well as sharing food, we can pray for opportunities to share spiritual counsel and the good news of salvation with those we serve.

If we encourage Christians who own businesses, shops, office complexes, farms, and stores to keep the church informed of their needs for temporary, part-time, and/or full-time workers, we can also develop a cooperative job availability information service for the unemployed. Local churches may begin such a service primarily for their own members, but they can extend that service to other needy members of their community and discover new ways to witness to non-Christians in the process. Although Christians cannot solve the national problem of unemployment, we should at least be able to care about, help and support each church family affected by unfavorable economic conditions.

And lay persons like you can have a key role in starting such caring ministries and motivating other Christians to act locally. A *Christianity Today* Gallup Poll found that while between 30 percent and 40 percent of both Catholic and Protestant clergy believe they should help the poor, less than one percent identified concern for the poor as one of their "especially successful" church programs.[4] This may be partly the result of the pastors' unwillingness to initiate potentially controversial social ministries in conservatively-minded churches. But lay people do not need to wait for theolog-

ical agreement in order to serve compassionately. We
cannot afford to let nonessential disagreements or different interpretations of biblical teachings prevent us
from doing something. In fact, lay men and women can
pioneer such ministries without provoking contro-
versy. As lay persons, let's work together in the strength
and unity that come from our common love for our Saviour.

We lay men and women who have heard God's call to
care for those in need must familiarize ourselves with
current needs in our congregations and communities.
Then we must do what we can to solve those problems
with the Lord's help. And we must motivate others to
act locally. Although the needs are great, church members who join hands and work together prayerfully can
expect God's blessing on such an effort. Lay men and
women must take the lead and pioneer this strategic
ministry because we have the best opportunities to
understand the problems of those who are struggling to
survive economically and spiritually.

Church leaders—pastors, elders, or deacons—cannot carry this load on their own. We must share the
responsibility and care for one another in the Christian
community. Each of us must ask, "Lord, what do you
want *me* to do? Lord, what do you want *my family* to
do? Lord, what do you want *my church* to do?"

Lay men and women with a God-given vision of caring for the needy members of their congregations can
begin such a ministry unobtrusively—one-to-one, fam-
ily-to-family. If you keep your church's pastor and leaders properly informed of your ministry goals, progress,
and effectiveness you will win their backing and blessing.

The way you begin a practical caring ministry in
your church may depend on the specific needs your
church members are wrestling with. In some communities, unemployment will be an obvious problem to
tackle first. In others, a caring ministry may spring

from a Bible study group, a hospital visitation program, or simply because one individual takes a special interest in unwed mothers, shut-ins, or mothers with pre-school children.

You can begin a caring ministry right where you are—in your church. You can use your existing resources, skills, and ideas to *do* what you can. Now!

For Study or Discussion

1. Have you personally observed areas in your local community where there is poverty? Have you ever thought of this as *your* problem? What one thing might you do this week for one poor family in your church or community?

2. When you hear of someone losing his or her job, is your first reaction: (a) Boy, I'm glad it's not me; (b) Well, I'll just have to pray for that family; (c) I wonder if I can help them with their rent or house payment or buy a couple of weeks' worth of groceries?

3. What is your church doing to alleviate material poverty in your local community? in your city? in the world at large? Is this enough? What more could you suggest that could be done? Be specific.

4. Read and discuss Isaiah 58:6-12 with a friend. Then write down a suggestion as to how you could personally apply this passage of Scripture.

5. Review Matthew 25:31-46. Describe what you learn from Jesus' words in one short sentence. Pray for opportunities to practice what you have learned.

6. Read 1 John 3:17-18 again, and reread John Stott's comments on page 26. What are some of the needs you see in the world today? How can you, or your church, do something to meet those needs?

Notes
1. Orlando E. Costas, *The Integrity of Mission*, (San Francisco: Harper and Row Publishers, 1979), pp. 70-71.
2. John Stott, *Christian Mission in the Modern World*, (Downers Grove, IL: Inter-Varsity Press, 1975), p. 28.
3. Harold O.J. Brown, "What's the Connection Between Faith and Works?" *Christianity Today*, October 24, 1980, pp. 26-29.
4. Robert T. Henderson, "Ministering to the Poor: Our Embarrassment of Riches," *Christianity Today*, August 8, 1980, p. 16.

Chapter 2
Biblical Guidelines for Caring and Sharing

Your church *can* care, your church *must* care! Caring ministries need caring *people*. Women and men just like *you*. Individuals whose hearts God touches. And we must base our caring ministries on biblical convictions, principles, and guidelines. The Apostle Paul, in his letter to Titus, one of his spiritual sons, stressed this need to develop caring individuals who will do good works.

Good Qualities for All Christians

By writing his short letter to Titus, Paul gave the church a profile of the qualities all Christians should aim for. Paul's letter to Titus will help you to encourage others to develop these practical qualities in their lives. Study Paul's message to Titus for yourself, then live out its practical teachings. Encourage those who join you in a caring ministry to apply the practical principles Paul gave Titus in your local church's ministries. Paul's letter to Titus includes just three chapters and forty-six verses. But every phrase in Titus contains intensely practical, action-packed principles for a caring lifestyle. You may be surprised to see the emphasis Paul puts on doing good, but you'll discover lots of encouragement for your caring ministry as you listen to the Apostle Paul's intense longing that Christians demonstrate the truth and relevance of the gospel through lives filled with good works.

Titus traveled with Paul and Barnabas to Jerusalem (Gal. 2:1), and probably accompanied Paul on some of his other travels. He was Paul's special representative in Corinth, and organized the collection for the poor Christians in Jerusalem (2 Cor. 8:3-6). He delivered Paul's second letter to the church in Corinth on his own initiative (2 Cor. 8:16-17). Paul calls Titus his "partner and fellow worker" (2 Cor. 8:23), and "Titus, my true son in our common faith" (Titus 1:4). After Paul's release from prison in Rome, Titus accompanied him to Crete. Paul left Titus in Crete to strengthen the new churches there by appointing elders and teaching the new converts sound doctrine and sound behavior.

Although you may tend to think of Paul as a theologian who didn't pay much attention to the practical aspects of Christianity, a careful study of his short letter to Titus shows that Paul expected every Christian to demonstrate the reality of his faith by living a good life and doing good works.

Paul instructs and encourages Titus to teach the Christian in Crete to live holy, attractive lives. Anyone appointed to lead God's work in a local church must live as a shining example of godliness. A church leader must live blamelessly, love what is good, encourage his fellow believers, and refute anyone who opposes sound teaching (Titus 1:7-9).

Paul reminds Titus to keep alert for "mere talkers and deceivers . . . [who] claim to know God, but by their actions they deny him. They are detestable, disobedient and unfit for doing anything *good*" (Titus 1:10,16, italics added).

Titus must teach the older men to be "sound in faith, in love and in endurance" (Titus 2:2). Older women, too, must be "reverent in the way they live," godly women, who can *teach what is good"* (Titus 2:3, italics added). Good life-styles are essential for good teachers. Their walk must match their talk (see Jas. 3:1).

As he teaches young men, Titus must *encourage* them, and Paul explains, "in everything [Titus must] set them an example *by doing what is good"* (Titus 2:7, italics added). Each Christian should live, "so that in every way they will make the teaching about God our Savior attractive" (Titus 2:10).

Above all, Paul reminds Titus to encourage the Christians on the island of Crete to develop attractive and productive life-styles because Jesus "gave himself for us to redeem us from all wickedness and to purify for himself a people that are his very own, *eager to do what is good"* (Titus 2:14, italics added).

Paul urges Titus to teach the believers how to live in society as well: "Remind the people to be subject to rulers and authorities, to be obedient, to be *ready to do whatever is good,* to slander no one, to be peaceable and considerate, and to show true humility toward all men" (Titus 3:1-2, italics added).

Then he goes on to remind Titus of the unbreakable link between salvation and service. Good works do not earn salvation, but salvation produces good works. Good Christians naturally learn to *do good.* A living faith produces a life devoted to good works. And such a life of service is one more result of the merciful salvation won by Christ's sacrificial death:

> When the kindness and love of God our Savior appeared, he saved us, not because of righteous things we had done, but because of his mercy.

He saved us through the washing of rebirth and renewal by the Holy Spirit, whom he poured out on us generously through Jesus Christ our Savior, so that, having been justified by his grace, we might become heirs having the hope of eternal life. This is a trustworthy saying. And I want you to stress these things, *so that those who have trusted in God might be careful to devote themselves to doing what is good.* These things are excellent and profitable for everyone (Titus 3:4-8, italics added).

In closing, Paul explains that every Christian must learn to do good. First, every able-bodied Christian must learn how to work for a living so he or she can support himself or herself and his or her family financially. Second, every Christian must be devoted to doing good works so his faith is not unproductive or self-centered. A productive faith will produce good works that meet the practical needs as well as the spiritual needs of others. Attractive Christian life-styles, the kind that will encourage non-Christians to consider Christ for themselves, combine faith and works. Throughout his letter to Titus, Paul aims to encourage Titus to help the believers become the good seed of the kingdom—women and men devoted to doing good as a natural outcome of a living faith in a living Saviour. Teach, encourage, and show your people how to live good lives and how to devote themselves to doing good at all times, writes Paul. "Our people must learn to devote themselves *to doing what is good,* in order that they may provide for daily necessities and not live unproductive lives" (Titus 3:14, italics added).

Paul's instructions to Titus will make a difference in your church if you train disciples to do good and care for others. Paul's teachings on good works reflect God's own concern for caring and sharing. God communicates His will throughout the Scriptures, and a thorough study of both Old and New Testaments will equip you to mobilize your congregation as a caring community of God's people in the world today.

The following selection of Scriptures shows how the Old Testament laws, Psalms and Proverbs, the prophets, Jesus, the New Testament apostles, and the New Testament church all taught the necessity of caring and sharing. While I've selected only some of the major Scriptures, many of the books included in the bibliography will give you more references and suggestions for further Bible study. Whether you study these passages as an individual, a small group, or a church, look for ways to apply what you learn. Correct belief must produce correct behavior. Act on what you learn, incorporate the biblical insights you discover into your lifestyle. Devote yourself to doing what is good at all times.

Old Testament Laws

In the Old Testament you'll discover many examples, principles, and laws for caring and sharing. Studying them in depth will give you a clearer understanding of how God wants you to minister to needy people. You'll see how He is equally concerned for insiders and outsiders. God cares for His own people, and He loves aliens and strangers. He cares equally for the members of the Christian community and those who are not yet members of the Christian community. As you study these exciting Old Testament Scriptures, look for ways to apply them in your local church's ministry today.

In the second book of the Bible God reminds His people that He hears the cry of all who are mistreated and oppressed, just as He heard the Israelites' groanings in Egypt (Gen. 6:5). The memory of God's concern for them during their bondage in Egypt must inspire His people to care for those who suffer. God's people must not take advantage of widows or orphans, nor can they charge excessive interest when loaning money to the needy. If a cloak is taken from someone as a pledge, it must be returned before sunset "because his cloak is the only covering he has for his body. What else will he sleep in? When he cries out to me, I will hear; for I am compassionate" (Exod. 22:27). Because God is compassionate, His people must exercise compassion in their daily affairs.

"Do not follow the crowd in doing wrong" (Exod. 23:2), God exclaims. His people must be willing to stand alone and do good. God's people must not deny poor people justice (Exod. 23:6), and because they know how it feels to live in a strange land, they must not oppress aliens (Exod. 23:9). God even told landowners they could only harvest their land for six years. In the seventh year, the poor were to be allowed to harvest crops for themselves (Exod. 23:10-11).

When Jesus taught His disciples to love their neighbors, He was restating an Old Testament law. In Leviticus 19:16-19, you'll discover that neighbor-love was one of the central laws God told Moses to give the Israelites: "Do not do anything that endangers your neighbor's life. I am the Lord. Do not hate your brother in your heart . . . . Do not seek revenge or bear a grudge against one of your people, but love your neighbor as yourself. I am the Lord. Keep my decrees."

In Leviticus 19:9-10, you'll also see how God emphasizes His special concern for the poor and aliens. "When you reap the harvest of your land, do not reap to the very edges of your field or gather the gleanings of your harvest. Do not go over your vineyard a second time or pick up the grapes that have fallen. Leave them for the poor and the alien. I am the Lord your God."

And in the Ten Commandments God reveals how

His people should relate to Him, how they should live in their families, and how they should interact with their neighbors (see Lev. 20:1-17).

Beginning with Old Testament laws like these, God explains how He expects His people to relate to the materially poor and those who've been forced to become aliens or refugees. The alien, the person from another country and culture who is living in a strange land, must be treated as kindly as any neighbor. "When an alien lives with you in your land, do not mistreat him. The alien living with you must be treated as one of your native-born. Love him as yourself, for you were aliens in Egypt. I am the Lord your God" (Lev. 19:33).

When Moses taught the people these laws, no doubt he remembered his own life in Egypt—where he grew up as a foreigner in Pharaoh's court. Moses even named one of his sons Gershom, a name which sounds like the Hebrew word for "an alien there" (Exod. 18:3).

Notice how these instructions are all emphasized with the phrase, "I am the Lord your God." God Himself cares for the poor, the alien, and your needy neighbor. He wants you to care for these individuals in the same loving way that He cares for them. Above all, as Moses' instructions to the people show, God wants everyone to be treated justly. "Do not pervert justice; do not show partiality to the poor or favoritism to the great, but judge your neighbor fairly" (Lev. 19:15).

In Leviticus 23:22 God repeats the law of gleaning, and in Leviticus 25 He describes the year of Jubilee. Although scholars do not know whether the year of Jubilee was practiced, Christians can learn how God wants natural resources shared by studying Leviticus 25. We can also learn how God wants us to care for each other because He says, "Do not take advantage of each other, but fear your God" (Lev. 25:17). In our society, the opposite standard often applies. People strive to take advantage of each other and completely ignore God's commands on caring for one another.

Christians living in a secularized society cannot impose Old Testament laws like God's instructions for the year of Jubilee in either the public or the private sectors of the economy. As Donald Kraybill notes in *The Upside Down Kingdom*, "Allowing wheat to stand every seventh year in Nebraskan wheat fields won't feed the hungry in New York or Bombay."[1] Yet, these Old Testament patterns can influence contemporary Christians' economic philosophies and policies. As Kraybill concludes, "The biblical model of Jubilee ought to be the economic norm within the corporate life of the church. And it provides a distinctly biblical perspective to guide the Christian community's behavior in the larger economic system."[2]

The last verses in Leviticus 25 give instructions on how to redeem anyone sold into slavery. God reminds His people they are all His slaves, all His servants. As His servants, they all belong to Him. They cannot live exclusively for themselves, they must live to serve and glorify the Lord their God (Lev. 25:55).

And so must we. God's Old Testament laws must guide, inform, and permeate our lives today. Although individually and corporately we no longer need to observe the letter of the Old Testament laws, we must inhale their spirit and do those things which please God. As Jesus said, "Woe to you, teachers of the law and Pharisees, you hypocrites! You give a tenth of your spices—mint, dill and cummin. But you have neglected the more important matters of the law—justice, mercy and faithfulness. You should have practiced the latter, without neglecting the former" (Matt. 23:23).

On another occasion, when Satan tempted Jesus to turn stones into bread during the forty-day wilderness temptations, Jesus quoted Deuteronomy 8:3. "Man does not live on bread alone but on every word that comes from the mouth of the Lord." Such Old Testament Scriptures as these speak to the needs of contemporary lay men and women. Deuteronomy 8 opens with God's explanation for the forty-year desert wanderings of the Israelites. "Remember how the Lord your God led you all the way in the desert these forty years, to humble you and to test you in order to know what was in your heart, whether or not you would keep his commands" (Deut. 8:2). As well as humbling His people, God filled them with hope. They knew He was leading them into a land flowing with milk and honey—the Promised Land. Through Moses, God described the beauty and bountiful productivity of the Promised Land. Springs, streams, and pools of water would refresh this land. All sorts of grains and fruit trees would grow in the land "where bread will not be scarce and you will lack nothing" (Deut. 8:9). So long as the people observe God's laws, He promises them His abundant blessing on every area of their lives. They must remember He is the sole source of their prosperity, however. "Otherwise, when you eat and are satisfied, when you build fine houses and settle down, and when your herds and flocks grow large and your silver and gold increase and all you have is multiplied, then your heart will become proud and you will forget the Lord your God, who brought you out of Egypt, out of the land of slavery" (Deut. 8:12-14).

In today's world, men and women easily become proud and forget that God is the source of their ability to produce wealth. As God warned His people in Moses' day, "You may say to yourself, 'My power and the strength of my hands have produced this wealth for me.' But remember the Lord your God, for it is he who gives you the ability to produce wealth, and so confirms his covenant, which he swore to your forefathers, as it is today (Deut. 8:17-18).

God clearly warns that a failure to humbly acknowledge His blessing may cause an individual or nation to forget Him and start worshiping false gods. Obeying God's commands results in His blessing, but disobedience may bring destruction (see Deut. 8:20).

God frequently restates the principle of the divine ownership of all natural resources to make sure His people understand how to live. "To the Lord your God belong the heavens, even the highest heavens, the earth and everything in it" (Deut. 10:14). Always, God reminds His people of His special concern for the poor and needy. Those who enjoy great material blessing cannot use their material assets to win spiritual favors. Rather, like God Himself, they must use their material resources to bless the poor and needy. "For the Lord your God is a God of gods and Lord of lords, the great God, mighty and awesome, who shows no partiality and accepts no bribes. He defends the cause of the fatherless and the widow, and loves the alien, giving him food and clothing. And you are to love those who are aliens, for you yourselves were aliens in Egypt" (Deut. 10:17-19).

Later, Jesus taught His disciples, "I tell you, use worldly wealth to gain friends for yourselves, so that when it is gone, you will be welcomed into eternal dwellings" (Luke 16:9).

Similarly, God expected His people to tithe their crops so the Levites, aliens, orphans, and widows would all receive enough food. Those who gave out of their produce would also receive God's blessing, "in all the work of your hands" (Deut. 14:29).

God told His people there should not be any poor people among them if they observed His commands faithfully. "There should be no poor among you, for in the land the Lord your God is giving you to possess as your inheritance, he will richly bless you, if only you fully obey the Lord your God and are careful to follow all these commands I am giving you today" (Deut. 15:4-5). Imperfect obedience meant there were poor people among the chosen people, so God told His people not to treat their poor hardheartedly or tightfistedly. "Rather be openhanded and freely lend him whatever he needs" (Deut. 15:8). God's people are commanded "to be openhanded toward your brothers and toward the poor and needy in your land" (Deut. 15:11).

Here again, the Old Testament provides clear guidelines for contemporary application. Christians must care for the poor within the Christian community, and we must care for the poor and needy within the society in which we live and work as well.

Employers are given similar instructions to actively work for the welfare of their employees in Deuteronomy 24:14-15: "Do not take advantage of a hired man who is poor and needy, whether he is a brother Israelite or an alien living in one of your towns. Pay him his wages each day before sunset, because he is poor and counting on it. Otherwise he may cry to the Lord against you, and you will be guilty of sin."

Refusing to pay hired workers, or even delaying a payment, is sinful in God's sight. James, the Lord's half-brother, restates this Old Testament theme in the thunderous language of a prophet in his warning to rich landowners: "Look! The wages you failed to pay the workmen who mowed your fields are crying out against you. The cries of the harvesters have reached the ears of the Lord Almighty" (Jas. 5:4). Hoarding wealth in the last days and living luxuriously and self-indulgently will bring nothing but weeping, wailing, and misery according to James.

Hannah, Samuel's mother, in her insightful prayer-song says the Lord sends both poverty and wealth. She also proclaims that He raises the poor to positions of honor:

The Lord sends poverty and wealth;
   he humbles and he exalts.
He raises the poor from the dust
   and lifts the needy from the ash heap;
he seats them with princes
   and has them inherit a throne of honor.
(1 Sam. 2:7-8).

Ruth, another Old Testament heroine, personally experienced the benefits of God's concern for poor foreigners when she gleaned the leftover grain in a field owned by Boaz (Ruth 2:2). After learning about Ruth's hard work in the fields, and her devotion to Naomi, Boaz invited Ruth to work alongside his servant girls and to drink from the water jars his men filled. When Ruth asked Boaz why she was given such favors, he replied, "I've been told all about what you have done for your mother-in-law since the death of your husband—how you left your father and mother and your homeland and came to live with a people you did not know before. May the Lord repay you for what you have done. May you be richly rewarded by the Lord, the God of Israel, under whose wings you have come to take refuge" (Ruth 2:11-12).

Boaz applied God's Old Testament commands by personally caring for Ruth, a foreigner. Later, he married Ruth. She bore him a son, Obed, who became the father of Jesse—King David's father. Boaz obeyed God's laws of gleaning and caring for aliens, and God blessed Boaz by giving him a wife. Eventually, one of their descendants was the Messiah (see Matt. 1:5-6).

Psalms and Proverbs
In their poetic and practical sayings, the Psalms and Proverbs reinforce many of the other Old Testament teachings on caring and sharing. The psalmists knew

that God observes human troubles and griefs. Anyone victimized by wrongdoers can commit their cause to God, for He is "the helper of the fatherless" (Ps. 10:14). God is both the encourager and the defender of the oppressed.

> You hear, O Lord, the desire of the afflicted;
>   you encourage them, and you listen to their cry,
> defending the fatherless and the oppressed,
>   in order that man, who is of the earth, may terrify no more (Ps. 10:17-18).

David also repeats the biblical basis for practicing a careful stewardship of all the earth's resources— including people, possessions, and natural resources. "The earth is the Lord's and everything in it, the world, and all who live in it" (Ps. 24:1). He is the sole owner, and we are His stewards. If we want His blessing on our stewardship, then we must be prepared to meet His demand to seek Him humbly for He is holy, "The Lord Almighty—he is the King of glory" (Ps. 24:10).

God's holiness is not limited to His character, however. His holiness influences His caring actions in the lives of hurting people. He is "a father to the fatherless, a defender of widows," who "sets the lonely in families" (Ps. 68:5-6). He listens to the prayers of a needy individual (Ps. 69:33), and stands at his right hand to save his life (Ps. 109:31).

Even the descendants of the man who worships the Lord and obeys His Word will experience God's blessing (Ps. 112:1-3). For "in darkness light dawns for the upright, for the gracious and compassionate and righteous man. Good will come to him who is generous and lends freely, who conducts his affairs with justice." (Ps. 112:4-5).

This kind of person shares the conviction David expresses in Psalm 140:12: "I know that the Lord secures justice for the poor and upholds the cause of the needy."

With all God's people, the psalmist lifts his voice in a song of praise which eloquently summarizes Old Testament teachings on the caring character and concerns of the Lord:

> The Maker of heaven and earth,
>> the sea, and everything in them—
>> the Lord, who remains faithful forever.
> He upholds the cause of the oppressed
>> and gives food to the hungry.
> The Lord sets prisoners free,
>> the Lord gives sight to the blind,
> the Lord lifts up those who are bowed down,
>> the Lord loves the righteous.
> The Lord watches over the alien
>> and sustains the fatherless and the widow,
>> but he frustrates the ways of the wicked
>> (Ps. 146:6-9).

In the first chapter of Proverbs, Solomon explains that one of his reasons for writing the book was to help his readers *do* "what is right and just and fair" (Prov. 1:3). Throughout Proverbs, Solomon inserts many principles and promises concerning the need to care for one another, especially the poor. Like many of the Old Testament writers, Solomon knew that God is intimately affected when His poor are mistreated. "He who oppresses the poor shows contempt for their Maker, but whoever is kind to the needy honors God" (Prov. 14:31; see Prov. 17:5 also.) The opposite is also true. God rejoices when the poor are treated kindly, "He who is kind to the poor lends to the Lord, and he will reward him for what he has done" (Prov. 19:17).

Even the person who neglects the needs of the poor may suffer when he needs help, according to Solomon. "If a man shuts his ears to the cry of the poor, he too will cry out and not be answered" (Prov. 21:13). Whether he is a rich tyrant or another poor person, anyone who deliberately oppresses the poor leaves a trail of destruction in his wake "like a driving rain that leaves no crops" (Prov. 28:3). Proverbs 28 includes a pointed warning to anyone charging too much interest: "He who increases his wealth by exorbitant interest amasses it for another, who will be kind to the poor" (Prov. 28:8); while the generous person will find encouragement in Proverbs 28:27: "He who gives to the poor will lack nothing." Showing kindness and acting generously is one way to help the poor, but Solomon goes further, instructing his readers that "the righteous care about justice for the poor" (Prov. 29:7) as well.

And the last chapter of Proverbs urges every Bible reader to "speak up for those who cannot speak for themselves, for the rights of all who are destitute. Speak up and judge fairly; defend the rights of the poor and needy" (Prov. 31:8-9).

The godly wife described in the same chapter is also a lover of the poor, "She opens her arms to the poor and extends her hands to the needy" (Prov. 31:20).

All of God's people can apply the teachings of Psalms and Proverbs on caring and sharing. No one can selectively claim the other blessings and promises described in these insightful books, however, without also obediently applying their practical principles for helping the poor and needy out of a simple, joyful, love for God—Maker of heaven and earth, Creator and Saviour, Lord and Master of both poor and rich alike.

Old Testament Prophets

The Old Testament prophets reminded God's people

of the specific ways they rejected His laws and teachings on doing right and caring for one another. Isaiah began his ministry, for example, by pleading with the nation to recognize that God does not listen to the prayers of those whose lives contradict their pious words:

> Take your evil deeds
>   out of my sight!
> Stop doing wrong,
>   learn to do right!
> Seek justice,
>   encourage the oppressed.
> Defend the cause of the fatherless,
>   plead the case of the widow
>   (Isa. 1:16-17).

Isaiah longed for his people to obey God's Word from the heart. He knew the spiritual leaders of his day were leading the people astray (Isa. 3:12).

Through Isaiah, the Lord announced His judgment against the elders and leaders of the nation. "'It is you who have ruined my vineyard; the plunder from the poor is in your houses. What do you mean by crushing my people and grinding the faces of the poor?' declares the Lord, the Lord Almighty" (Isa. 3:14-15).

Isaiah's contemporaries put their concern for their own pleasure ahead of their personal relationship with God. "They have harps and lyres at their banquets, tambourines and flutes and wine, but they have no regard for the deeds of the Lord, no respect for the work of his hands" (Isa. 5:12-13), says the prophet. In spite of the people's failure to recognize God's handiwork, God's faithful servant tells them, "The Lord Almighty will be exalted by his justice, and the holy God will show himself holy by his righteousness" (Isa. 5:16).

Consistently, Isaiah proclaims God's judgment on

the oppressors of his day: "Woe to those who make unjust laws, to those who issue oppressive decrees, to deprive the poor of their rights and rob my oppressed people of justice, making widows their prey and robbing the fatherless" (Isa. 10:1).

Isaiah turns his people's attention to the coming of the Messiah who will be filled with the Spirit of God, and who will delight in the fear of the Lord: "With righteousness he will judge the needy, with justice he will give decisions for the poor of the earth" (Isa. 11:4). Isaiah's sharp prophetic vision enabled him to see the distant time when, as a result of the Messiah's coming, "The earth will be full of the knowledge of the Lord as the waters cover the sea" (Isa. 11:9).

His moving, unforgettable portrait of God's suffering Servant in Isaiah 53 still challenges God's servants everywhere to learn from the Messiah's willingness to give Himself for the salvation of mankind. Though our service cannot match His, we must model our servanthood after His selfless pattern of loving service. We can learn more about how to minister to God's needy children by prayerfully reflecting on Isaiah's moving description of the Saviour.

"He was despised and rejected by men . . . familiar with suffering" (Isa. 53:3). He "carried our sorrows" and was "crushed for our iniquities . . . and by his wounds we are healed" (Isa. 53:4-5). From a human viewpoint, the Messiah's ministry appeared as though it would end tragically. But, as Isaiah was privileged to see by faith, "It was the Lord's will to crush him and cause him to suffer" (Isa. 53:10). God turned an apparent defeat into victory. One man's death purchased salvation for all mankind. God justified many sinners as a result of His Servant's sacrificial death, and rewarded Him for His service: "Therefore I will give him a portion among the great, and he will divide the spoils with the strong, because he poured out his life unto death, and was numbered with the transgressors. For he bore the sin of many, and made intercession for the transgressors" (Isa. 53:12).

All who personally know God's suffering Servant as their Saviour ought to gladly walk in His footsteps. His followers will even battle injustice and oppression in the power of His Spirit (Isa. 58:6). They will feed the hungry, shelter the poor, and clothe the naked (Isa. 58:7; see 61:1-6 also). Those who follow the Servant-Saviour will see God fulfill His promise:

> If you spend yourselves on behalf of the hungry
> and satisfy the needs of the oppressed,
> then your light will rise in the darkness,
> and your night will become like the noonday.
> The Lord will guide you always;
> he will satisfy your needs in a sun-scorched land
> and will strengthen your frame.
> You will be like a well-watered garden,
> like a spring whose waters never fail
> (Isa. 58:10-11).

Isaiah's prophetic, prayerful message is still relevant for lay persons who will make themselves available to serve God in their local churches today. If you want God to use you to begin a caring ministry in your local church, then pray along with Isaiah:

> Since ancient times no one has heard, no ear has perceived, no eye has seen any God besides you, who acts on behalf of those who wait for him. You come to the help of those who gladly do right, who remember your ways . . . you are our Father. We are the clay, you are the potter;

we are all the work of your hand . . . . Oh, look
upon us, we pray, for we are all your people (Isa.
64:4-5,8-9).

Jeremiah, too, shared Isaiah's concern that the people of his day should demonstrate God's justice in all of
their interpersonal relationships, especially by showing
a practical concern for aliens, orphans, and widows.
Jeremiah also reminded his people that knowing God
includes defending the poor and needy (see Jer. 7:5-7).
And Ezekiel noted four reasons why God judged the city
of Sodom so severely, "She and her daughters were
arrogant, overfed and unconcerned; they did not help
the poor and needy" (Ezek. 16:49).

Amos, one of the shepherds of Tekoa—a town in
Judah, about ten miles south of Jerusalem—was not
trained in any of the schools for prophets. Yet Amos's
preaching ministry was firmly based on his God-given
conviction to demand righteousness and justice from
the people of the Lord in the name of the Lord. Amos
was especially concerned with the social sins of Israel
(Amos 2:6-7).

He criticized Israel for exploiting the poor instead of
caring for them (Amos 5:11), and explained how the
people should change their life-styles.

> Seek good, not evil,
>   that you may live.
> Then the Lord God Almighty will be with you,
>   just as you say he is.
> Hate evil, love good;
>   maintain justice in the courts
>   (Amos 5:14-15).

Amos predicted that the Lord would send Israel into
exile because of the nation's obsession with profit-mak-
ing at the expense of the poor (see Amos 8:4-6).

Amos, the working man who herded sheep and

tended sycamore trees, spoke for the Lord in his day. A strong love for the Lord inspired him to stand for God even though his countrymen were more interested in buying and selling than worshiping and obeying their Creator. Amos spoke for all of the Old Testament prophets when he said, "Let justice roll on like a river, righteousness like a never-failing stream!" (Amos 5:24).

Frank Gaebelein's concluding paragraph in "Old Testament Foundations for Living More Simply," in *Living More Simply*, explains how to relate Old Testament Scriptures to obedient discipleship today:

> The Old Testament does not tell us specifically whether we should buy a better car, keep the one we have or have no car at all. It does not tell us whether we should upgrade our lifestyle by getting a bigger house, or cut it back by getting a smaller one. It doesn't specify exactly what our lifestyle should be. Rather, it gives us certain principles by which we must measure our lifestyle. To face those principles honestly and prayerfully is bound to lead to changes that will help us simplify our lives in order to be more obedient disciples of our Lord.[3]

And Stephen Charles Mott, professor of Christian Social Ethics at Gordon Conwell Theological Seminary in South Hamilton, Massachusetts, comments:

> To those who wonder about the Christian use of such Old Testament passages, it must be pointed out that this justice cannot be restricted to the Old Testament or to any one period, covenant, or dispensation. It precedes, succeeds, and transcends the Israelite theocracy and is the basis of the contemporary Christian social ethic.[4]

Jesus

Jesus began His public ministry by announcing in the synagogue at Nazareth that God would use Him to fulfill the prophecy recorded in Isaiah 61:1-2. Jesus said that God's Spirit had anointed Him "to preach good news to the poor . . . proclaim freedom for the prisoners and recovery of sight for the blind, to release the oppressed, to proclaim the year of the Lord's favor" (Luke 4:18-19).

A careful study of Jesus' ministry reveals that He brought both spiritual and physical healing to those He ministered among. Today, our ministries must follow His example. We must bring the good news of salvation that changes lives, and we must do the good works of mercy that will heal the hurts of those who suffer. Proclaiming the gospel for our times must include a Christ-like concern for both the body and the soul.

When Jesus called the first disciples to follow Him, He challenged them to leave behind the security of steady work, their possessions, a regular income, and their families (see Matt. 4:18-22). He called them to follow Him in a life of faith that included learning from Him while serving spiritually lost and physically sick people. In the process of teaching and preaching the good news of the kingdom, Jesus took His disciples among the people. As He healed all kinds of diseases and sicknesses, the disciples received a firsthand introduction to the pain and hopelessness of human suffering. Jesus discipled His followers in the midst of the real world. And so must we.

Like Him, we must take our discipleship into the streets. If our gospel is only seen and heard by those who gladly attend Sunday services in a well-decorated sanctuary, then it is not the same gospel that Jesus shared with those "ill with various diseases, those suffering severe pain, the demon-possessed, the epileptics and the paralytics" (Matt. 4:24). Jesus' disciples learned the art of caring and sharing by watching the Saviour share His life in a caring ministry that excluded no one.

If we will open our hearts and minds to His Word today, He will teach us the same lessons so that as caring lay persons we can motivate our fellow believers to act locally for Jesus' sake.

If you want to care for others Jesus' way, begin by reading Matthew 5–7. Then look for opportunities to live out His teachings in your home, in your neighborhood, and in your local church. As you read Jesus' words you'll discover how all-inclusive His love is and how He wants all of His followers to keep on meeting needs in His strength.

Jesus taught His disciples to live such good lives that others would immediately recognize the extraordinary ways in which His followers demonstrated their faith. Instead of letting worldly standards govern their conduct, His disciples' lives should surpass reasonable, socially acceptable codes of behavior. "Let your light shine before men, that they may see your good deeds and praise your Father in heaven" (Matt. 5:16).

Unlike the Pharisees and teachers of the law, Jesus' disciples must practice what they preach. Those who teach without translating theory into concrete action may not enter the kingdom of God (Matt. 5:19-20). In many areas of life, Jesus' disciples will surprise their contemporaries by their generosity and their willingness to do more than just enough to get by (Matt. 5:38-42).

Jesus' expectations always exceeded the minimum legal requirement. "You have heard that it was said, 'Love your neighbor and hate your enemy.' But I tell you: Love your enemies and pray for those who persecute you, that you may be sons of your Father in heaven" (Matt. 5:43-45). As Luke noted, Jesus taught His followers to "Be merciful, just as your Father is merciful" (Luke 6:36).

Jesus reminded His disciples to pattern their conduct on their heavenly Father's love for all people. He does not discriminate by blessing only those who observe His laws. "He causes his sun to rise on the evil and the good, and sends rain on the righteous and the unrighteous" (Matt. 5:45). If God loves everyone, His followers ought to love everyone in the same way.

> If you love those who love you, what reward will you get? Are not even the tax collectors doing that? And if you greet only your brothers, what are you doing more than others? Do not even pagans do that? Be perfect, therefore, as your heavenly Father is perfect (Matt. 5:46-48).

Clearly, Jesus expects His people to do more than others. Real maturity results in a life that cares for others and shares with them just as abundantly as God cares and shares.

You may think that Matthew 6 is so packed with challenging teaching that it will take a lifetime to apply it all. But you can start an exciting life of faith today by applying just one principle from this rich chapter from the Sermon on the Mount. For example, try seeking His kingdom and His righteousness first in all you do today (Matt. 6:33).

As you study Matthew 6, notice how Jesus assumes that all of His disciples will give to the needy (Matt. 6:1-4), and live prayerful lives of faith (Matt. 6:5-34). Jesus expects His disciples to pray, give, and practice a life of faith. And in Matthew 5–7 He describes the qualities and principles that will enable you to learn God's values and personally practice a kingdom life-style.

Jesus promised His disciples that God would reward their generosity. "Give, and it will be given to you. A good measure, pressed down, shaken together and running over, will be poured into your lap. For with the measure you use, it will be measured to you" (Luke

6:38). And He gave His disciples opportunities to exercise their faith and learn how God provides (see Luke 9:1-6).

If you want to become spiritually rich, do not store up material resources for yourself. Instead, learn to live in genuine dependence on God for your needs, and generously share your spiritual and material resources with others.

> And do not set your heart on what you will eat or drink; do not worry about it. For the pagan world runs after all such things, and your Father knows that you need them. But seek his kingdom, and these things will be given to you as well. Do not be afraid, little flock, for your Father has been pleased to give you the kingdom. Sell your possessions and give to the poor. Provide purses for yourselves that will not wear out, a treasure in heaven that will not be exhausted, where no thief comes near and no moth destroys. For where your treasure is, there your heart will be also (Luke 12:29-34).

As you learn from Jesus, remember that He demonstrated His teachings in a life of service. Let His example motivate you to live and act for His glory. "For you know the grace of our Lord Jesus Christ, that though he was rich, yet for your sakes he became poor, so that you through his poverty might become rich" (2 Cor. 8:9).

Remember, too, as you get out where the needs are and begin caring for people and sharing your love and faith and resources with them, that you are ministering to Jesus. As Mother Teresa says, when you look into the faces of God's needy, you see Him "in His distressing disguise." One day, when you meet your heavenly King, He will greet you by name and say, "Whatever you did for one of the least of these brothers of mine, you did for me" (Matt. 25:40).

Let Jesus' identification with the poor, hungry, thirsty, sick, needy, and imprisoned call you into His service in your local area today. "For I was hungry and you gave me something to eat, I was thirsty and you gave me something to drink, I was a stranger and you invited me in, I needed clothes and you clothed me, I was sick and you looked after me, I was in prison and you came to visit me" (Matt. 25:35-36).

New Testament Church

New Testament churches applied the biblical teachings on caring and sharing within their local communities. The early Christians were expected to demonstrate the reality of their faith by their deeds (Acts 26:20). And they did.

Together, the believers learned how to care for each other while the apostles taught them the Word of God. Prayerfully, generously, and sacrificially they met each other's needs. As they met together, worshiped together, and fellowshiped together, God blessed their testimony and multiplied the disciples in Jerusalem (Acts 2:42-47). Because they "shared everything they had" (Acts 4:32), Luke—a careful historian—could report, "There were no needy persons among them" (Acts 4:34).

Key verses like Acts 2:45 and 4:34 describe "repeated acts of sharing whenever there was a need rather than one automatic transfer of all possessions to a common purse," according to the introduction to Acts 4:32-37 in *Cry Justice.*[5]

The quality of life observed among the Christians in Jerusalem was soon reproduced among the believers in many other cities around the Mediterranean as well. Paul taught the Christians at Rome that the spiritual transformation of their lives would result in unconventional and nonconformist living within the Body of Christ. He urged the saints in Rome to use their gifts cheerfully, diligently, and generously in loving service to one another: "Be devoted to one another in brotherly love . . . . Do not be overcome by evil, but overcome evil with good," (Rom. 12:10,21) wrote Paul.

The churches in Galatia also learned to care for their members' needs and to do good to all people. "Therefore, as we have opportunity, let us do good to all people, especially to those who belong to the family of believers" (Gal. 6:10).

During his extensive missionary travels Paul personally experienced every imaginable kind of hardship, from stoning to hunger (see 2 Cor. 11:23-29). But in the midst of such extreme difficulty, he learned the secret of facing all sorts of circumstances in the strength that God supplies. As he told the church at Philippi:

> I have learned to be content whatever the circumstances. I know what it is to be in need, and I know what it is to have plenty. I have learned the secret of being content in any and every situation, whether well fed or hungry, whether living in plenty or in want. I can do everything through him who gives me strength (Phil. 4:11-13).

Paul learned the secret of contentment in the school of deprivation. Real-life experience shaped his theology and permeates his writings. The early churches grew and multiplied because they learned to live by faith no matter how few their resources or how frightening their circumstances. Outstanding church planters like Paul lived out their faith in a hostile world, and ordinary Christians followed their leaders' courageous examples.

Paul urged Timothy to teach that "godliness with contentment is great gain" (1 Tim. 6:6). Paul insisted that Timothy must teach Christians to put their hope in God rather than their wealth. Paul also expected rich Christians to care for others and do good by sharing their resources. "Command them to do good, to be rich in good deeds, and to be generous and willing to share" (1 Tim. 6:18). The writer to the Hebrews also encouraged his readers to be content and to remember God's promise never to abandon them (Heb. 13:5-6).

James wrote emphatically to Jewish Christians about their need to prove the reality of their faith in Christ by works and deeds that resulted from their belief in God.

> What good is it, my brothers, if a man claims to have faith but has no deeds? Can such faith save him? Suppose a brother or sister is without clothes and daily food. If one of you says to him, "Go, I wish you well; keep warm and well fed," but does nothing about his physical needs, what good is it? In the same way, faith by itself, if it is not accompanied by action, is dead (Jas. 2:14-17).

The New Testament church leaders, the apostles, all expected their church members to demonstrate the reality of their faith by doing good works, by caring for one another, and by sharing their resources with both fellow believers and needy non-believers. The Apostle John sums up the practice of the New Testament churches when he writes, Whoever claims to live in him must walk as Jesus did (See 1 John 1:6-7). And John left his readers in no doubt about just how to practically live, walk, love and serve as Jesus did.

> Jesus Christ laid down his life for us. And we ought to lay down our lives for our brothers. If anyone has material possessions and sees his brother in need but has no pity on him, how can

the love of God be in him? Dear children, let us
not love with words or tongue but with actions
and in truth (1 John 3:16-18).

For Study or Discussion

1. Although we as Christians are no longer under
the Mosaic Law we live by a greater law—the law of love!
Read Deuteronomy 14:28–15:11. Which of these commandments could you apply to your world today, under
the law of love? How can you personally observe these
commandments?

2. The law of love is also expressed in James 2:1-8.
Read this passage and consider your obligation under
the law of love.

3. If you need further motivation to give to those in
need, read Malachi 3:10-12 and Luke 6:38. In these
passages God says to *prove* Him and see if it will not be
personally, materially rewarding to give.

4. Select one Old Testament verse or passage from
this chapter and paraphrase it in your own words. Per-
sonalize the verse or passage you select—apply it to
your own life and ministry.

5. Choose one of the New Testament teachings on
caring and sharing, then discuss it with someone you
know. In what ways is the teaching you selected relevant for Christians today?

6. Summarize what you have learned about the biblical guidelines for caring and sharing in a short paragraph. Pray through your summary statement every
day for a week.

Notes
1. Donald Kraybill, *The Upside Down Kingdom*, (Scottdale, PA: Herald Press, 1978), p. 111.
2. Ibid, p. 111.
3. Frank Gaebelein, *Living More Simply* (Downers Grove, IL: Inter-Varsity Press, 1980), pp. 38-39.
4. Stephen Mott, *Biblical Ethics and Social Change* (New York: Oxford University Press, 1982), p. 61.
5. Ronald J. Sider, ed., *Cry Justice*, (Downers Grove, IL: Inter-Varsity Press, 1982), p. 61.

Chapter 3

Use Existing Resources

"Pastor," I said nervously, "I'm calling because I'd like to share an idea a group from the church has . . . ."

All week long I'd been wondering how my pastor would respond when I called. What would he think of me wanting to work in the area of social and physical needs? Would he check my theology, question my qualifications, or just say he was too busy to get involved?

"This is an answer to prayer," he said after listening attentively. I then asked him to attend our caring group's first meeting. He replied, "For some time now I have been praying with some of our elders that someone in the church would start a ministry like this. When do you meet? I'll put it on my calendar. Thanks for calling. I'll be praying for your new ministry."

A few days earlier I'd sent a rough draft of our group's plan and purpose to our pastors for their review. Since my pastor had already read the background information, he was eager to support us. I'd also written a letter to our board of elders simply stating what we hoped to accomplish.

Our Christian life-style class's attendance averaged around thirty each week. Although the interest in starting some kind of action group to follow up the class seemed strong at first, I wondered how many would come to the first organizational meeting. About twenty people, including two of our pastors, came! This was more than I expected, and enthusiasm ran high. Our discussion included brief explanations of what we hoped to do that evening (we wanted to agree on our purpose and goals if possible) and a brief time of sharing ideas and trying to answer questions. The pastor I'd called so nervously the week before was one of our most enthusiastic participants. He suggested some practical guidelines which were written into our group's guidelines right away.

Paul, one of the lay people at our first meeting, made an important suggestion. "I've been reading in Acts lately," he said, "and I wonder if the 'Barnabas Group,' after Barnabas—the disciple who was such an encourager—might fit." Paul's suggestion caught on right away. The Barnabas Group was born!

A study of Barnabas's interesting biography confirmed we had a meaningful name to live up to. Luke introduces Barnabas in Acts 4:36-37. "Joseph, a Levite from Cyprus, whom the apostles called Barnabas (which means Son of Encouragement), sold a field he owned and brought the money and put it at the apostles' feet."

Although Barnabas may have been a recent convert at that time, Luke singles him out as an outstanding example of the commitment and generosity of the Christians in Jerusalem. Luke contrasts Barnabas's willingness to sell his field and give all of the money he earned to the apostles with the deceitfulness of Ananias and Sapphira (Acts 5:1-11).

Because the church in Jerusalem was blessed by the dedication and generosity of members like Barnabas, "There were no needy persons among them" (Acts 4:34). Barnabas's ministry of encouragement blessed the apostles—the church leaders—and his generosity supplied practical help to the poor members of the Jerusalem church. He was a real spiritual leader in the world's first local church. As Luke comments later in Acts, Barnabas was "a good man, full of the Holy Spirit and faith" (Acts 11:24). Barnabas combined a personal ministry of evangelism and disciple-making with a willingness to share his material resources with poor believers in Jerusalem. In Antioch, Barnabas taught the believers the necessity of sharing their resources with their poor brothers and sisters in Christ.

He also encouraged Saul when the other apostles were not ready to accept the newly converted Saul's testimony. As the two ministered together in Antioch, and when they later traveled together as missionaries, Barnabas initially set the pace. Paul learned more about the Lord, the Scriptures, and how to evangelize and disciple others as he sat at Barnabas's feet. Working side by side, Saul observed Barnabas's generosity and together they encouraged the Christians in Antioch to send financial aid to the Christians in Jerusalem. When Barnabas and Saul presented the gift to the Jerusalem church, the Jerusalem elders asked them to "continue to remember the poor" (Gal. 2:10).

And Barnabas's ministry of encouragement included his cousin John Mark as well. When Paul and Barnabas argued over John Mark's earlier decision to return to Jerusalem—instead of continuing on with Barnabas and Paul during their first missionary journey—Barnabas accepted John Mark. He took him with him to Cyprus while Paul traveled with Silas on his second missionary journey.

Later Paul commends Mark as a useful co-worker. Thanks to Barnabas's sensitive ministry of encouragement, Paul and Mark were eventually reconciled.

Mark later wrote the earliest gospel—the Gospel of Mark. Barnabas's other disciple, Paul, went on to write most of the New Testament during his extensive letter-writing ministry to individuals and churches. The lives and ministries of both men were strengthened, at key times in their growth and development, by Barnabas—the encourager.

Barnabas enriched the Church of Jesus Christ for all time by encouraging both John Mark and Paul. His ability to minister to individuals blended with his concern for strengthening and building up local congregations. His inspiring ministry combined a ministry of personal evangelism and disciple-making with a concern for the welfare of the Christian community. Personal ministry and social ministry were equally important in the work of Barnabas, the Son of Encouragement.

As we launched a new caring ministry in our local church, we knew his name would always remind us of the importance of encouraging one another in the work of the Lord.

How the Barnabas Group Started

Although our name came out of a home meeting one Friday evening, the Barnabas Group itself grew out of a weekly adult elective Sunday School class. For twelve weeks we studied the Scriptures together, read Ron Sider's *Rich Christians in an Age of Hunger* and discussed various topics related to our theme—"Christian Life-style in a Changing World."

The class members who wanted some kind of ongoing group had deep biblical convictions. Even before the class started, many of them were already thinking, praying, and acting out their faith to help those with real needs. And as we prayed and shared together during the fall and winter of 1979 we developed close personal relationships. The group members' biblical convictions, plus strong interpersonal friendships, laid the basis for an effective ministry.

If you want to begin a caring ministry, evaluate the availability and maturity of potential group members carefully. If you already have a small group whose members (1) know each other well, (2) have deep personal roots in the Scriptures, and (3) are already demonstrating initiative in meeting needs, you may be ready to start a new caring ministry right away.

But if you are not sure that you have the right combination of spiritual maturity and enthusiasm, be patient. Perhaps a Sunday School class, home Bible study, or a short series of small-group discussions will help you to identify a band of caring individuals who share your vision. Look for those in your church who are already doing something in the areas you are interested in working. Talk to those couples and individuals. Share your heart, pray together, and trust the Lord to bind you together into a caring ministry team for Him. Share your hopes with your pastors and the lay leaders of your church, and ask them to pray for you also. You may be the answer to their prayers!

You may learn that some small groups are already doing a good job meeting individual needs. But often any existing groups will have another primary purpose—Bible study, prayer, or fellowship. If so, your church may still need someone who would think in terms of coordinating a church-wide caring ministry. Other friends and members may be especially interested in reaching out into the local community with Christ's love. Find out what others are interested in doing, listen to the ways God's Spirit is already working in your church members' hearts and lives, and adjust your plans to include anyone who shares your vision. The people among whom God is already working will be one of your most valuable resources. And one of the best ways to make use of that existing resource is to brainstorm your ministry together.

Brainstorm Your Ministry

Once you have identified your potential ministry group members, spend some time together brainstorming your purpose and goals. Brainstorming is a creative planning process that should be applied frequently to ministry opportunities because it lets everyone share ideas and helps shape a group's ministry.

The guidelines for brainstorming include: (a) the more ideas the better; (b) no criticism—record *every* idea suggested (evaluation comes later); (c) hitchhike on others' ideas—one idea sparks another.

And it's usually best to limit the amount of time spent brainstorming a topic to about thirty or forty-five minutes per topic.

After you have covered as many ideas as possible, then you can evaluate and prioritize your ideas. Brainstorming is useful in planning because it produces more ideas in less time than any other method. As you begin a new ministry and do creative planning, brainstorming will help you make the best use of your time. You can refine your first draft later. As your ministry progresses, you may want to brainstorm specific problems or projects. You may vary the size of the brainstorming group to draw on different individuals' strengths and creativity.

The leader or facilitator of a brainstorming session has a key role. He or she must explain the ground rules for brainstorming, and then clearly define the topic the group will work on. The group leader must be ready to guide the group, suggest new directions, and draw out the quieter participants. It's usually best to have someone else recording the results on a chalkboard, tackboard, or large newsprint pad so the ideas can be seen by all of the participants. Some groups use 5 x 7 or 3 x 5 cards. Each group member is given a supply of cards to write on, and the cards are then pinned up on charts or walls to create a storyboard from the brainstorming session. This approach has the advantage of making later review easier. The cards can be left up, and they can be rearranged easily when you begin prioritizing ideas.

When you have written the first draft of your caring ministry's purpose and goals, remember that it's only a *draft.* Don't get too attached to any pet projects, ideas, or even the wording of your statement of purpose. A draft is just a draft. Circulate it to all those whose input you want, and to those whom you need to keep informed about your ministry's progress. Some of your best plans and most helpful guidelines will come back as feedback from those who review your first draft. Circulating a draft plan also involves more people in the planning process. The more people who feel they have given advice or suggestions, the better. Their involvement in these early stages will make it easier for you to explain your group's ministry and to recruit their assistance later on.

Your statement of purpose and goals should also include some guidelines for your ministry. No ministry team can accomplish everything. You are part of a local body, encourage the other members to do their functions also. And strive to work together. Like Barnabas, be a pacesetter and an encourager. Don't take over existing ministries if all they need is a little encouragement to revive them and give them new life and direction. Model a caring life-style in all of your interaction with other ministries and ministry leaders in your church. Sharpen the focus of your ministry so you won't conflict with others, and encourage people to join other ministry teams and serve in other groups in your church also.

As the Barnabas Group worked on our statement of purpose we went through several drafts, each one shorter and simpler than the previous one. We wanted a simple statement that would communicate the purpose of our ministry, and enough guidelines so we would not need to call a committee meeting every time we needed to make a decision. We were committed to the idea of using existing resources, and wanted to avoid reinventing the wheel wherever possible. If someone else or another group in the church already had a way to handle a need, we would not necessarily do anything except refer someone to that source of help.

Sample Purpose and Guidelines
Here's the revised version of the Barnabas Group's purpose:

> To stimulate the implementation of caring ministries at Pulpit Rock Church through:
> —identifying and communicating needs
> —personal example
> —coordinated group efforts
> —coordinated church-wide efforts.

Three years after this purpose statement was written and revised, we are encouraged by how well each aspect of it has been accomplished in some way or another.

The introduction of our ministry helped emphasize the need for church members to care for one another. In the past our church had often been characterized as a large, unfriendly church. Although our group cannot claim responsibility for changing the church's atmosphere and reputation, we are one of many groups that had a direct influence on improving the warmth and friendliness of our members. Existing relationships were deepened, and new friendships started. Simply getting church members together to talk about needs and what could be done about them encouraged many—both directly and indirectly—to start new personal or small-group ministries.

Many small Bible study groups and care clusters extended practical, financial, and material help when their group members experienced financial difficulties, unemployment, family problems, or other forms of stress. The birth of the Barnabas Group provided one resource network that was not limited to any particular small group. We would help anyone, whether they were in an existing ministry group or not. Our church staff now had a lay-led resource group which they could call on when there was no other way to meet a specific need. And we expected our group members to take the initiative in identifying and meeting needs within our body also.

Sample Caring Ministry Guidelines

The practical strategy which still guides our thinking developed as a result of intensive Bible study and discussion with our Christian life-style class. We also talked to other laypeople, tried to read up on what others were doing, and shared our ideas with our own pastors and leaders. The following guidelines were a result of many suggestions, and we refined the ideas and advice we were given to match our church and the goals of our members:

1. Focus on local ministry—Pulpit Rock Church and Colorado Springs community (approximately 75 percent time and effort)

2. Include occasional, short-term involvement with national or international projects (approximately 25 percent time and effort)

3. Avoid duplicating existing church ministries and community agencies

4. Emphasize caring and sharing with existing resources by stressing personal involvement rather than financial gifts

5. Make no cash handouts

6. Convene monthly growth/support group—for prayer, teaching, communication, coordination, and sharing

7. Maintain decentralized approach to needs identification and resolution to simplify procedures and encourage individual initiative.

These guidelines included both our philosophy of ministry and some practical procedures. As well as outlining these general principles we included a description of whom we would work with. We put this section of our guidelines under the heading *Who Qualifies for Help?* Our list attempts to suggest an order of priority, and relates directly to guidelines 1 and 2. Interestingly, our ministry has followed the suggested patterns of involvement quite closely in practice. Here's our description of whom we wanted to serve:

1. Members of Pulpit Rock Church
2. Attenders of Pulpit Rock Church
3. Friends and contacts of our members and attenders
4. Selected community (Colorado Springs) needs and projects
5. Non-church (national/international projects) selected to educate and mobilize church-wide participation.

Identifying Needs

As well as stating our purpose and describing some guidelines for our ministry, we also listed four ways of identifying needs:

1. Pastoral referrals
2. Member referrals
3. Barnabas Group members' referrals
4. Small-group ministries' referrals.

In most churches, the pastoral staff will often be the first to become aware of needs. Your church office staff may receive calls from friends of those with special needs also. By forming a group with the primary aim of ministering to those with physical and social needs, you will help your church staff by providing them with a resource network to turn to when they become aware of specific needs.

But, above all, make sure your caring group members become the primary eyes and ears for your ministry. Encourage them to look and listen, to become sensitive, caring observers. By asking occasional polite questions you'll be able to check up on individuals and families in your congregation. The more involved your ministry group members become in the life of your church, the more regularly you will be able to help meet needs.

When you first start your caring group, publicize its existence to your church. If people know your group exists, they can refer needs and call upon you when help is needed. But the effectiveness of your ministry will depend upon your members' commitment to reach out, love, and serve the church as a whole. You must take the initiative, you must care, you must make the connections with those who are hurting.

Too often, finances are the first need mentioned by someone thinking about starting a new local church-based ministry. In difficult economic times, church budgets are put on hold. Fund-raising schemes are not welcomed immediately if many members are underemployed or unemployed. Finance committees search for ways to trim unnecessary expenses; they don't try to think up more ways to spend money. Therefore, a new caring ministry that uses only existing resources—people, time, and finances—will receive a warm welcome. But a group that asks for special funding won't necessarily find much encouragement.

Determine to use only existing resources for your ministry. Everyone can rearrange their schedule so they can give some time to a caring ministry. You'll be surprised to discover how much can be done by recycling furniture, appliances, clothing, tools, and other items. Don't let a tight budget prevent you from sharing what you have to share. God doesn't want you to give what you don't have, but He does want you to share your surplus.

Can I Do It?

While writing our guidelines, we emphasized the importance of personal commitment to the caring ministry. The statement of purpose and the guidelines are useful, but they are only guides. A caring ministry depends upon the commitment, availability, initiative, and action of those who take part in the ministry. Your most important guideline will be a simple series of three questions which will help each member of your caring ministry decide when and how to meet any specific need he or she encounters. I've used these questions personally in almost every caring project I've tackled, and I've encouraged others to ask them of themselves whenever they see or hear about a specific need or project. The three questions are:

1. Can *I* do it?
2. Can I do it *now*?
3. Can I find *someone else* to do it?

If you can meet a need by using your skills and resources, do it! Occasionally your schedule will make it impossible for you to do something right away. That's when you ask yourself, "Can I find *someone else* to do it?" Ask the third question when you personally are not able to meet the need.

By using the combined resources, skills, talents, and gifts of your congregation, there's very little you won't be able to do. One wintry day I received a call from my wife. A friend had called to ask for help in an emergency. One of her elderly neighbors, a lady who lived alone in a mobile home, had a desperate problem. Her water pipes had frozen, and the severe winter storm meant she couldn't go out for help by herself. After turning to our church directory to search for anyone employed as a plumber, another friend provided an immediate solution. One of the local agencies working with the elderly in our city already had an emergency service for such problems. They were only too willing to mend the frozen pipes. With just a few phone calls, we were able to take advantage of existing resources by locating a local service agency that was organized and staffed to handle the situation. I'm not even a handyman, let alone an experienced plumber, so I would have been unable to help that lady in the specific way she needed help. And my work schedule would have prevented me from reaching her right away. But by searching for someone else with both the time and the skills to do the job, I was able to help match a solution with a specific emergency need.

Another friend purchased an old but large home so he and his wife could provide a home for unwed mothers. When we first visited Steve's home to hear about this new ministry, it looked as though his vision surpassed the available resources. The home would need a lot of work before his ministry could become a reality. He needed to remodel the second floor almost completely. It was the kind of project I wouldn't plan to tackle myself. But a brief description of the need was all it took for two skilled craftsmen, Mike and Bob, to decide they would lend a hand if the necessary materials were provided. And they did. Because of their deep commitment to the Lord and their willingness to donate their talents to a worthwhile ministry, the remodeling has been completed and several unwed mothers have stayed in Steve and Barbara's home.

How to Inventory Skills and Resources

In order to use existing resources, you must know what they are. So you'll find it helpful to inventory the skills and resources of those who join your caring ministry, and maybe even those of your whole congregation.

Design a simple one-page form and make copies for everyone. With the arrival of microcomputers and word processors in some church offices and homes, you may be able to keep the records of your talent/skills/resource bank on computer. Encourage those who complete the form to include all of their talents—whether or not there's an immediate need for those talents. The Barnabas Group Inventory Form (see figure 1) includes personal information, resources, and activities the individual is interested in.

BARNABAS GROUP PERSONAL INVENTORY

LAST NAME_____ FIRST NAME_____ DATE_____

ADDRESS_____ ZIP_____

HOME PHONE_____ WORK PHONE_____ BIRTHDATE_____

CHILDREN_____ BIRTHDATE_____

_____ _____

_____ _____

_____ _____

RESOURCES AVAILABLE

☐ Time   AM_____   PM_____   WEEKEND_____

☐ Vehicles   Car_____   Truck_____   Trailer_____   Other_____

☐ Home   Spare Room_____   Storage Space_____   Group Mtgs_____

☐ Tools   Yard Equipment_____   Woodworking_____   Other_____

☐ Clothing   Age_____   Size_____

☐ Furniture

☐ Food

☐ Other _____

ACTIVITIES YOU CAN DO

☐ Letter writing   ☐ Phone calling

☐ Visitation   ☐ Secretarial work

☐ Child care   ☐ Yard work

☐ Household maintenance   ☐ Car maintenance

☐ Friendship   ☐ Hospitality

☐ Teaching Sunday School   ☐ Leading Bible study

☐ Shopping   ☐ Transportation

☐ Housekeeping   ☐ Political Activity

☐ Counseling--Type_____   ☐ Professional Advice/Resource
                                  Type_____

☐ Skills/Hobbies_____

_____

Comments:_____

_____

Figure 1

Anyone joining the church can be asked to complete the form and return it to the church office. If every church maintained such an inventory of all the members' resources, talents, and interests, and used the available resources regularly, it would dramatically reduce the number of unmet needs in local churches. Design a form that suits your congregation.

Of course, the key to making such an approach functional, is knowing where to find the necessary information when you need a specific resource person. One way is to include the occupations and professions of your members in your church directory. Our church recently compiled a small-group directory in which we tried to identify every small group that anyone in our church took part in regularly. Having an up-to-date list of all the ministry leaders in the church provides another helpful source for locating resource people.

An emphasis on using existing resources, and a decentralized approach to finding and meeting needs gives everyone a ministry. Every small group, every Bible study, every Sunday School class, every craft or recreation class should be encouraged to seek to meet needs within its membership. When a problem is too large for the small group to handle by itself, your church-wide caring ministry can help. If there's an established, functioning network of caring people in your church you can call on many of them to become involved in problem solving. You can also communicate information and help to make needs known. Many people will be delighted to help someone else if only they know there is a need they can meet. Your best work as a caring ministry will often be communicating needs and stimulating others to get personally involved in applying Paul's encouragement to "carry each other's burdens, and in this way you will fulfill the law of Christ" (Gal. 6:2).

Referrals

While you will be able to handle most of the physical and social needs your group members encounter, there will be some cases you cannot handle. Some personal problems require professional counseling, and other difficulties can best be handled by specialized groups and/or professional counselors. As well as becoming thoroughly familiar with your own church's resources, you should get acquainted with all of the counseling and other resource networks available in your local community through other local churches and social service agencies. Most communities will have directories which you can circulate among your pastoral staff, church office staff, and key small-group leaders in your church.

The Colorado Springs HELP-Line Referral/Resource Handbook, for example, includes over 250 local, state, and national telephone numbers for various emergency needs. Agencies and resources for alcoholism, the aged, child abuse, emotional and mental health, drugs, marital and family problems, various hot lines including life support and rape counseling, runaways, crash houses, military human resource centers, food services, runaways, employment, legal, and other resource groups and agencies are all included. Our police department's chaplaincy corps also makes a wallet-sized card available, listing forty-four local referral telephone numbers for handy reference.

Locate similar agencies in your community and incorporate them with your caring group's own resources. You can also make the information available to your church staff who often receive calls from people in need of immediate assistance. If such directories and referral lists have not been compiled yet in your particular community, take the initiative to research what services are available and compile your own list. Share it with other churches, ministries, and community agencies as well.

Procedures for Providing Emergency Assistance

When the economy slows down and unemployment rises, the number and the severity of emergency needs multiply. Churches that formerly never dealt with human needs find that some members are out of work and having difficulty paying their rent or mortgages, and some are having a hard time feeding their families. Churches that are accustomed to dealing with emergency needs, and already have food pantries and other existing social assistance programs, find they become swamped with demands for assistance. Whatever the dimensions of the problem in your local church, try to develop some systematic procedures for interviewing those with needs when that is an appropriate way to verify and meet those needs. While some churches will be able to meet most needs on an informal basis, many will discover that individuals or families with recurring problems, transients, or non-members from the community at large can be served only if orderly, fair, routine procedures are established and used by those who have responsibility for this ministry.

While the specific approach will vary from church to church, an interviewing process should include the following:

1. Respect for the dignity of each person you seek to help
2. Confidentiality
3. Orderly, efficient interview procedures
4. A written record of each interview, including the type of assistance provided
5. Training for the interviewers, when possible.

One of the reasons for keeping written (or computerized) records is simply to discourage anyone from abusing the system. Your church interviewer can easily fill out a form such as the sample in figure 2 in the course of a brief interview. Your church secretary, receptionist, or emergency needs committee member can also

RECORD OF REQUESTS FOR EMERGENCY NEEDS

DATE	NAME OF CALLER	# IN FAMILY	SOC. SEC. #	PHONE #	WALK-IN	TYPE OF NEED				
						FOOD	CLOTHES	SHELTER	EMER. $	OTHER

Figure 2

use such a form to assist with record-keeping.

When you initiate procedures for meeting emergency needs in your church, develop guidelines and get them approved by the church leadership first. Although our Barnabas Group does not give cash handouts, our local church does provide occasional financial assistance to members and friends with legitimate needs. We have an "Elders' Fund" just for this purpose. Members and attenders may give directly to the fund, and occasional special offerings also help replenish it.

While gifts to needy members or friends were often handled informally in the past, we are now moving toward setting up a small committee to administer the fund and interview those with needs who have asked for assistance or been referred to the committee. Often these needs are first mentioned as prayer requests, or someone in the congregation brings a specific need to the attention of either a pastor or an elder who then arranges an appointment to meet with the individual or couple, if possible. The gifts to members from the fund are outright gifts, and no repayment is required. Most are one-time or occasional gifts since most of those we help are able to recover quite quickly. However, if an individual or family has a recurring need the committee may elect to arrange for some voluntary work around the church as a way of matching the extra assistance with voluntary service.

While the Elders' Fund gives us a church-wide "safety net," we continue to emphasize the priority of meeting practical needs on a personal and small-group basis. Recently, we have also become involved as a church in a cooperative church ministry which provides emergency needs counseling and assistance to residents of a specific geographic area in our city. If we are unable to meet a need by using our own church resources, we can refer needy persons or families to the cooperative ministry for an appointment. This cooperative emergency service is staffed by volunteers from cooperating churches, and funded by voluntary monthly contributions from participating churches and individuals.

As well as providing immediate emergency assistance, the caring church will also provide spiritual, vocational, marital, and other forms of counseling to those in need. Often an emergency need is just a symptom of more complex personal problems. The unemployed need emotional support and spiritual direction as well as financial aid. Others will need help if their marriage relationship is suffering because of money problems. The caring church will do all it can to provide a total counseling and support environment. Lay counselors, informal support groups, and caring individuals who will give their friendship to those struggling with personal crises are all needed. No matter what it costs in terms of time and effort, the local church is the best institution for helping and supporting individuals or families in crisis. The church needs "good Samaritans" who care.

And often the best way to care is to use existing resources rather than create new ministries or programs. Survey the existing resources—especially people, time, and finances—within your congregation, pray, and plan to use all of those available resources to meet needs practically and effectively. And as you begin using your existing resources more effectively, remember to encourage each person involved with your caring ministry and your local church's ministries, to keep on asking these three simple questions whenever they learn about a particular need:

1. Can I do it?
2. Can I do it now?
3. Can I find someone else to do it?

For Study or Discussion
Think about the following questions in your personal study or discuss them in your group:

1. The author gives three characteristics for group members of a caring ministry. Name them. Do these characteristics fit you and/or each member of your group?

2. Using the guidelines for brainstorming, spend some time talking about your purpose and goals. List everything that comes to mind or that is mentioned in your group. Follow the rest of the author's instructions for prioritizing your goals and pinpointing your purpose as a caring group.

3. How will you and your group become aware of needs in your community? List some resources you now have available.

4. List some needs you know about right now and apply the "three questions" to each need.

Chapter 4

Wanted: Servant-Leaders

"John, this is Bill. Sorry to be calling you so late, but I'm leaving town for the weekend tomorrow morning. So I won't be able to set up the display. Would you mind doing it instead?"

Two weeks earlier, Bill had agreed to handle all of the details—but now, at the last minute, he was announcing he simply couldn't do the project.

John felt discouraged. Bill seemed to have the commitment, caring heart, and the abilities needed to do an excellent job of helping to lead this growing ministry. But now John and his wife would have to make all of the arrangements instead.

What happened? As John and Mary discussed the reasons for their last-minute scramble to handle the preparations, they concluded that Bill wasn't quite ready to assume a leadership role in the ministry. He seemed to have all of the qualities needed in a caring ministry leader, but he backed out on short notice. Although they had both discussed all of the necessary arrangements, John had hoped Bill would do the project on his own. Instead, Bill simply left for the weekend.

Disappointments like this will happen when you

start caring for people, leading a team, and trying to involve others in a caring ministry. Teamwork takes lots of communication, hard work, and a willingness to encourage and help each other.

Although John was disappointed by Bill's unwillingness to assume the leadership, he still thought of Bill as a vital member of the caring group. Bill loves the Lord, and cares deeply about the people who are overlooked and neglected by others. He has many exceptional God-given talents, and uses them frequently to serve others. Later, when Bill and John discussed the reasons why Bill had not taken the initiative and completed the project, John learned that Bill thinks of himself as a follower rather than a leader.

John learned an important lesson—don't assume that someone else is ready to lead. He resolved that in the future he would specifically discuss whether a person in his ministry wanted to take responsibility for a project before assigning it to them. Some may be able to take the ball and run with it, but most potential leaders need some coaching in the art of leading. Help them grow into positions of leadership rather than forcing them to lead.

In this book I've emphasized the importance of organizing and carrying out a caring ministry with lay persons. Lay men and women can effectively lead such a ministry because God has gifted the lay members of the body with the spiritual and practical gifts needed for ministries of social service and caring. Seminary training isn't an essential prerequisite for caring. Anyone can demonstrate concern for brothers and sisters in Christ in practical ways. In many cases, you will be able to identify those who have caring hearts because they will already be ministering to others on their own—unobtrusively, but effectively in many cases. If you know these people already, you may be able to begin a caring ministry simply by bringing them together. While they may still prefer to do some of their caring individually, remind them that they will be able to accomplish far more by working with a team of caring individuals.

While it is best for the leadership of your caring ministry team to come from your church's members, do not exclude the pastoral staff from your ministry. Explain to your pastor and other church leaders that you are willing to carry the burden for the ministry, to do the necessary planning, organizing, leading, and work. This allows the pastors and leaders to give themselves to their primary responsibilities—prayer, study, evangelism, preaching, teaching, visitation, and other pastoral concerns.

When the twelve apostles learned that the Greek-speaking widows were being neglected in the daily distribution of food in the first-century Jerusalem church, they wisely selected lay leaders and delegated that special service to them. Notice how the church leaders made sure their local church cared for its members' spiritual *and* physical needs. The apostles were set apart to *serve the Word,* and some of the leading lay men were set apart to *serve food* to the members of the Jerusalem congregation.

> The Twelve gathered all the disciples together and said, "It would not be right for us to neglect the ministry of the word of God in order to wait on tables. Brothers, choose seven men from among you who are known to be full of the Spirit and wisdom. We will turn this responsibility over to them and will give our attention to prayer and the ministry of the word" (Acts 6:2-4).

Interestingly, the disciples selected some of their best men for the assignment. The Seven were spiritually mature individuals. As lay men, they were known for their faith, wisdom, and the indwelling presence of the Holy Spirit in their lives.

While the apostles gave themselves to prayer and the ministry of the Word as church leaders, they also made sure the daily distribution of food would be handled by godly, mature, Spirit-filled individuals. The distribution of food was not a "second-class" ministry that could be handled by just anybody.

Stephen's example makes this especially clear. As Luke comments, "Stephen, a man full of God's grace and power, did great wonders and miraculous signs among the people" (Acts 6:8). Although he was one of those selected to feed the Greek widows, Stephen's personal ministry influenced many people. He was a godly man. He was also persecuted for his faith.

Even then, when his opponents turned up the heat and argued with him, "they could not stand up against his wisdom or the Spirit by which he spoke" (Acts 6:10). Stephen's magnificent speech to the Sanhedrin (see Acts 7:1-53) matches Peter's powerful preaching in its persuasiveness, though he was called primarily to serve tables, not to preach in public. After speaking to the Sanhedrin, Stephen looked up to heaven and saw Jesus at God's right hand. For the third time in two chapters, Luke observes that Stephen was "full of the Holy Spirit" (Acts 7:55). Finally, he was dragged out of the city and stoned while a young man named Saul looked on. Like Jesus, Stephen died praying for the forgiveness of his killers.

While the apostles concentrated on their specialized calling to preach and pray, spiritually mature lay people like Stephen concentrated on meeting physical needs within the local church. Both ministries were necessary, and the leaders of both groups were spiritually mature individuals. What did the two groups—the apostles and the Seven—have in common?

Both groups were devoted to serving others in Jesus' name. The believers served one another, and the church grew. During His earthly ministry, when the apostles lived with Him, Jesus constantly demonstrated and taught the priority of serving. After Jesus' death and resurrection, the Holy Spirit began multiplying the disciples in Jerusalem and reminded them of the importance of servanthood. The apostles and lay members of the church served one another in love. In the new Christian community, Christlike servanthood characterized the lives and ministries of both the leaders and the lay men and women.

Today caring churches need leaders and lay people who will gladly serve one another just as the apostles and the Seven served one another and the people in the Jerusalem church. We must rediscover the biblical priority of serving one another in love.

Christlike servanthood must once again become the central feature of our discipleship. Our churches must be led by prayerful teachers who share the leadership with wise, Spirit-filled, lay people. As you plan a caring ministry in your local church, study the apostolic church as Luke describes it in Acts. Prayerfully set apart lay men and women for the ministry of caring to complement your church's emphasis on prayer and the ministry of the Word. Like the Jerusalem church, your congregation will grow and multiply as the Spirit of God uses your faith, service, and witness to spread the Good News in your community.

When the Jerusalem church balanced the teaching of the Word with serving bread to needy members of the Christian community, the church grew by leaps and bounds. As Luke comments, "So the word of God spread. The number of disciples in Jerusalem increased rapidly" (Acts 6:7). The faithful preaching of God's Word equips disciples to serve one another in practical ways. And when church members serve one another and help meet each other's needs, the pastors and teachers are free to devote themselves to prayer and to studying and teaching God's Word. Both kinds of ministry are needed in local churches. And both ministry teams need Christlike, Spirit-filled, servant-leaders.

As a lay person who is either starting or leading a church-based caring ministry, make sure you involve both leadership groups in your ministry.

First, *involve lay leaders*—men and women who take personal responsibility for planning and carrying out the ministry. The members of this group will be actively and regularly involved in the caring ministry. Second, *inform your local church leaders*—the recognized spiritual leaders in your congregation. This group may include elders, deacons, pastors, or other spiritually mature men and women. While these individuals may be occasionally involved in some of the projects you do, you should aim to keep them regularly *informed* about your activities. Do not try to involve this group in all of the details of carrying out your ministry.

While the first group *executes* the caring ministry, the second group *endorses* the caring ministry within your local church. The proper involvement of both groups of leaders will insure the effectiveness of your work.

In a small church (with 150 members or less), you may need only the approval of your pastor. But generally the wisest approach includes describing your ministry to your church board and asking for their approval and blessing. Welcome your board's input and request their approval as soon as you have a group of men and women who are ready and eager to launch a new caring ministry.

Make every effort to become a vital part of your church's existing ministries. Get to know the leaders of other small groups and classes in your church, and keep them informed about ways they can occasionally become involved with your ministry team. Share your group's vision, and encourage the other group leaders in their specialized ministries also.

Keeping your church leaders properly informed of

your activities is more than a formality. Regularly sharing what you are doing, who's working with you, and what you are accomplishing will help make your group a well-known ministry resource. Since your pastor and other leaders will often be the first to hear about specific needs in your fellowship, you must initiate regular opportunities for interacting with them. An occasional written report (perhaps once a quarter), can be another helpful way to make your ministry a recognized part of your church's life and witness. By becoming part of both formal and informal communication networks in your church, you will learn of opportunities to serve and find more ways to make others aware of your group's resources and capabilities.

If you are planning to start a caring ministry in your church, and want to explain your ministry to your church's leaders and relate it to other existing ministries, these guidelines may help:

1. Describe your ministry in writing (include relevant Scriptures).
2. Explain *why* you want to start this new ministry.
3. Briefly list the names of key group members.
4. Explain how you will finance your ministry.
5. Describe any specific projects you plan to do.
6. Relate your small group's ministry to your church's mission, purpose, or goals.
7. Ask for the prayers, counsel, and approval of your church leaders.
8. Invite your pastor and/or other key leaders to take part in your first group meeting.

Keeping others well-informed about your activities will also help you to attract and recruit more people for your ministry. If your church leaders know what you are doing, they can also encourage gifted, motivated, and concerned men and women to help you. If your church has classes for new members, see if you can explain your work to each new class during the year. And if there is a greeters' program for regularly contacting visitors, you have another recruiting tool. All kinds of small groups, classes, and ministry teams can supply you with information about needy individuals and families within your church and community. So build effective, two-way communication links with your church's pastor, office staff, other ministry leaders, and as many of the members of your local body as you can. You may find another useful source of volunteers for your ministry in any parachurch groups which are active in your city. And some parachurch organizations may be willing to share information and staff specialists to help train and mobilize your local church's caring ministry.

As a layperson, your personal example will be your best means of influencing both the pastoral leaders and the lay leaders in your church. When both groups observe your commitment to serving, both groups will welcome your input. When they see the results of your personal and small-group ministries, they will recognize your ministry and encourage others to join you. In many churches the professional church staff and lay leaders are already overloaded. The laborers, workers, and volunteers needed for church ministries are still as scarce today as they were in Jesus' day (see Matt. 9:36-38). But your prayers and personal action can help change that. By demonstrating a genuine commitment to serving others, you will display the kind of spiritual leadership that is one of the greatest needs in local churches today. The loving, caring, practical spiritual leadership that's needed in our churches must come from the lay men and women—the ordinary members of the churches. Superstars are not needed. Golden-tongued preachers are not needed. But ordinary, Spirit-filled, caring individuals—men and women just like you—who are devoted to the Lord and His work are needed.

You *can* help to make a difference in your church by becoming a servant. Christlike servant-leaders are needed today more than ever before. If you'll lead others by serving, your ministry will accomplish far more than if you concentrate your efforts on getting recognition for your church work.

Servant-leaders are disciples who follow their Servant-Lord's own example. Servant-leaders willingly do anything He calls them to do. Servant-leaders care more about meeting others' needs than having others minister to them. Like Jesus, you can become this kind of servant. Like the women who helped Jesus throughout His earthly ministry, you can help to advance the Kingdom of God by your practical service to others. Like the Seven, your serving can free others to preach and pray. Like Barnabas, your Christlike service can inspire and train others to follow Jesus wherever He leads them. Like the Good Samaritan you can help those in your community whose needs are overlooked. Like many of the lay leaders in the first century church, your service can help build your local congregation into a united body whose ministry God empowers and enriches. Servant-leadership is costly, but the results will make the price you pay seem insignificant.

The following biblical examples of servant-leadership will equip and enable you to lead by serving. As you study the related Scriptures, ask God to give you a heart to serve in your local church. As He motivates and helps you become a Christlike servant, you will lead by serving. And as you model the servant life-style personally, many others will also decide to give their lives in service for Jesus Christ.

Jesus' Teachings on Servanthood

Jesus' teachings on servanthood, as seen in His actions and explained in His conversations, will also guide you in your service for Him. Jesus demonstrated servanthood throughout the three brief years He spent personally training the Twelve. The one lesson they would never forget was Jesus' personal example of serving others. Because He also served them, they knew He expected them to serve their fellow believers.

Jesus called the Twelve to be "with him" (see Mark 3:13-15) twenty-four hours a day. The Twelve were "with him" constantly. For three years they learned from the most faithful Servant the world has ever known. The lessons of servanthood that Jesus taught the Twelve were applied by the Jerusalem church. And we must apply the same lessons within our local churches today.

Jesus redefined the meaning of true greatness when He said,

> You know that those who are regarded as rulers of the Gentiles lord it over them, and their high officials exercise authority over them. Not so with you. Instead, whoever wants to become great among you must be your servant, and whoever wants to be first must be slave of all. For even the Son of Man did not come to be served, but to serve, and to give his life as a ransom for many (Mark 10:42-45).

The lesson for servants today is the same as it was then. If you want to be a Christlike leader, do not expect to be served. Do not hope that your ministry will be recognized, or that you will be rewarded for your service. Decide instead to serve others just as Jesus chose to serve you. Then you'll discover the joy of leading (and learning) by serving.

The Twelve may have learned most about servanthood on that unforgettable evening when Jesus wrapped Himself in a towel and washed their dusty feet. The disciples all waited for someone else to do the dirty-but-necessary work. To their surprise, their Lord gladly, voluntarily did the work of a house-servant. Then He used the real-life drama to teach them that servanthood is not an option, or just an occasional duty, but the personal responsibility of each of His disciples at all times:

I have set you an example that you should do as I have done for you. I tell you the truth, no servant is greater than his master, nor is a messenger greater than the one who sent him (John 13:15-16).

Slowly, Jesus' teachings on servanthood sank in. The disciples learned that leaders must be Christ's servants. They must lead by serving—by doing even the most menial tasks joyfully. They will even serve self-sacrificially, just like their Lord. He willingly came to earth to sacrifice His life for all mankind. Jesus confirmed the disciples' calling to a life of service by sending them out with the words: "As the Father has sent me, I am sending you" (John 20:21). Above all, *you* are sent to serve.

The Women Who Served Jesus

The example of many women who served Jesus still inspires women and men everywhere to devote their gifts and their lives to the service of the Lord Jesus, His church, and all of His people. Servanthood provides equal opportunities for women and men. Although the Twelve were all men, many women served alongside them. Some of these women also served the Lord in the local church at Jerusalem. For centuries, many Christian women from all walks of life have led the way in modeling the art of servanthood.

After describing Jesus' crucifixion, Matthew turns his readers' attention to the women who served Jesus. "Many women were there, watching from a distance. They had followed Jesus from Galilee to care for his needs. Among them were Mary Magdalene, Mary the mother of James and Joseph, and the mother of Zebedee's sons" (Matt. 27:55-56). These women cared for Jesus' needs, and their example can encourage you to serve Him today by caring for His people's needs in your local church.

Although the Twelve men had apparently fled in

fear, the women remained with Jesus in His darkest moment. Their courageous service shows how dedicated, caring disciples can serve their Lord. Like them, you can serve Him in the midst of life's most depressing circumstances.

These faithful women also shared the early church's commitment to prayer. Describing one of the apostles' gatherings for prayer in a room somewhere in Jerusalem, Luke writes, "They all joined together constantly in prayer, along with the women and Mary the mother of Jesus, and his brothers" (Acts 1:14). These women, who knew and served Jesus personally, were soon joined by other gifted women who dedicated themselves to serving their Saviour.

Barnabas—Serving by Encouraging Others

As we've already seen, Barnabas, the Levite from Cyprus, was well-known for his ministry of serving in the early church by encouraging others. His name means "Son of Encouragement," and he lived up to it. His life reveals many of the basic qualities of a Christlike servant. While his single most important contribution to the church's global mission may have been his discipling of Paul, Barnabas's encouraging ministry of serving others formed the foundation for his lasting personal influence in Paul's life.

When many Greeks began turning to the Lord in Antioch, the church in Jerusalem sent Barnabas to visit the new believers there. Luke tells us that Barnabas was glad to see the evidence of the grace of God at work in the new believers' lives. So he "encouraged them all to remain true to the Lord with all their hearts" (Acts 11:23).

Luke then paints a clear portrait of God's servant Barnabas: "He was a good man, full of the Holy Spirit and faith" (Acts 11:24). Barnabas's character, openness to God's Spirit, and a willingness to live by faith made him a model servant. These qualities of life shaped his actions and gave him the unique opportunity to become Paul's personal tutor in servanthood as well as many other aspects of discipleship.

Local churches today need men and women who will learn from Barnabas and prayerfully look for ways to encourage one another just as Barnabas encouraged the new believers in Antioch.

A study of Barnabas's life reveals a challenging description of a servant in action in the life and ministry of a local church. Clearly, Barnabas was an outstanding individual in his local church. Luke refers to his willingness to sell his land and give the proceeds to the apostles as an example of the generosity and willingness to sacrifice that characterized the Jerusalem church. A man of property, and possibly a recent convert, Barnabas made Christ Lord of his possessions as well as his person.

Barnabas's willingness to let the church leaders use the proceeds from the sale of his land made him an obvious choice for the mission to Antioch. The apostles in Jerusalem knew he was a trustworthy, reliable disciple. In Antioch Barnabas showed he was open to new movements of the Spirit, able to relate to people of another culture, and eager to encourage the first members of a new church. His own joy in the Lord overflowed, through his ministry of encouragement, to the new believers. Because Barnabas was a good person, he was able to do good to others. Because he was full of the Holy Spirit and faith, he could show others how to walk in the Spirit and live by faith. Luke adds that "a great number of people were brought to the Lord" (Acts 11:24), and it's likely that Barnabas's teaching ministry played a key role in introducing these men and women to personal faith in Christ. Barnabas was trained to evangelize the unsaved and he knew how to follow up the newly saved.

His unique ministry to the Apostle Paul would never have happened if Barnabas had not been the first

Christian to welcome the recently converted Saul into the Christian community. Everyone else was afraid of Saul, "But Barnabas took him and brought him to the apostles. He told them how Saul on his journey had seen the Lord and that the Lord had spoken to him, and how in Damascus he had preached fearlessly in the name of Jesus. So Saul stayed with them and moved about freely in Jerusalem, speaking boldly in the name of the Lord" (Acts 9:27-28).

When Saul's life was threatened in Jerusalem, he went home to Tarsus. Barnabas later traveled to Tarsus to bring Saul back to Antioch to resume his personal ministry to him. He encouraged Saul in the faith while they spent a year together. But before very long, Saul (now known as Paul, Acts 13:9) became the chief spokesman for their missionary team. Not everyone could have handled an apparent demotion as gracefully as it appears Barnabas did. His humility helped him view the change constructively. Barnabas was committed to using his disciple-making skills in the context of a team ministry. When they began ministering together, Barnabas set the pace for Saul. Later, Paul became the pacesetter for many local congregations. Gradually, less is heard about his mentor—Barnabas, but Paul's worldwide ministry would never have been possible without him.

One incident from their ministry in Antioch suggests the decisive influence Barnabas had in Paul's life. When the disciples in Antioch sent famine relief to their brothers and sisters in Jerusalem, was it because Barnabas had taught them the principle "each according to his ability" (see Acts 11:29)? Certainly, Barnabas practiced that principle when he sold his land and gave the proceeds to the apostles (Acts 4:36-37).

Notice, also, that the church selected Barnabas and Saul to take their gift to their sister church. No doubt Barnabas explained to Saul the Christian's responsibility for sharing with the needy while teaching the Christians in Antioch and during their trip to Jerusalem together. In Galatians, while recalling his visit to Jerusalem, Paul notes the church leaders there "asked . . . that we should continue to remember the poor, the very thing I was eager to do" (Gal. 2:10). Where did Paul's eagerness to help the poor come from? Surely from his personal tutor, Barnabas.

Barnabas, the servant who always encouraged others, demonstrated humility, generosity, and a willingness to let others take the lead. He was a pacesetter. Make him your pacesetter as you follow his example and strive to serve and encourage others today!

Joe Simmons, who pioneered the ministry of The Navigators in Australia and New Zealand, is another model pacesetter whose personal example made a lasting impact on my life. At a summer training program for collegians which I attended in 1969, Joe spoke on "Pacesetting." His description of the essential qualities of a pacesetter, as I've adapted them here from the notes I took on his message, suggest seven ways you can practice pacesetting as you lead others in a caring ministry in your local church:

1. *A pacesetter helps others reach their maturity in Christ.* He draws out the very best in another person to help him pass the pacesetter (Acts 9:27; 11:25-26; 13:1-2).

2. *A pacesetter leaves a pattern others can follow,* but they must stretch themselves if they want to keep up with the pacesetter.

3. *A pacesetter needs to be a step ahead (not miles),* but he or she must be a man or woman on the move—growing in grace and the knowledge of Christ (2 Pet. 3:18).

4. *A pacesetter listens to his coach.* He listens to God daily while praying, and while reading or studying the Word of God.

5. *A pacesetter aims for the finishing line.* He avoids disqualification by knowing the rules and run-

ning his race according to the rules (1 Cor. 9:27).

6. *A pacesetter follows Christ.* He is totally dedicated to Christ and lives in complete dependence upon Him (Gal. 2:20; 1 Cor. 10:31–11:1).

Servant-leaders—pacesetters—men and women who will follow the example of Barnabas and the women who served Jesus will help to make your caring ministry a fruitful one. Look for individuals who display the qualities of a pacesetter when you are looking for someone to fill a leadership role. And encourage others to grow spiritually and to become more skillful in the practical aspects of servanthood. Caring ministry leaders must lead by serving.

Such men and women will demonstrate a heart for the caring ministry, and the skills to do it. They will take initiative, be willing to work behind the scenes, and complete any assigned responsibilities as well as those they volunteer to do.

As you become more experienced in the ministry of caring, train others to help lead the ministry. Share what you have learned. "Tell them why, show them how, and get them started" as caring ministry leaders. Training others will be much easier if you make a note of things you learn about your caring ministry as you do it. Write up lessons learned, procedures, and general information that will help others to lead the ministry effectively. Share your life with those you train, and encourage them to ask you for help as they begin to assume leadership roles and responsibilities.

As noted already, you must also work at informing your church staff and/or board. The primary need here is to inform your church leaders about your ministry, not to try to involve them in specific projects. This approach will free them to concentrate on their primary ministries. As your ministry develops, regularly share what you are doing with your church staff and leaders. A brief conversation or a phone call will help to keep the lines of communication open between you and your church leaders. But every quarter or so it might be wise to write a one-page report on recent caring ministry accomplishments or projects. Sharing information regularly with your church leaders is just another way of serving them and your church. And as a caring ministry leader, you must model servant-leadership in all aspects of your life and ministry.

For Study or Discussion

1. Reread the guidelines the author gives for explaining your idea for a caring ministry to the church leaders. Now briefly describe or discuss these eight points.

    a. How would I describe this ministry?

    b. Why is it needed?

    c. Who are the leaders of the ministry?

    d. How will it be financed?

    e. What are some specific projects?

    f. How does this ministry fit our church's mission, purpose, or goal?

    g. Have I asked for the prayers, counsel and approval of the church leaders?

    h. Have I invited my pastor (and other church leaders) to participate in the group meetings?

2. In Mark 10:42-45 Jesus defined true greatness. What did He say? What did He mean in a practical way?

3. How does the pastor and/or the leadership team in your church view the need for the kinds of practical caring ministries described here? Make an appointment to discuss this question with a pastor or another lay leader in your church.

4. List the names of caring people who are already meeting needs in your church, and pray regularly for their ministries.

5. Review these questions and your answers, and then write out an action plan to follow through in one area of ministry.

Chapter 5

Do One Church-Wide Project

Once you have a *vision* for the kind of caring ministry you plan to do, a *method* for meeting needs, and the *approval* of your church's pastors and leaders, think about tackling *one church-wide project*. This will accomplish three basic objectives—you will (1) meet a specific need, (2) establish the identity of your caring ministry as one of the ministries of your local church, and (3) recruit more volunteers for your caring ministry team.

Why do a church-wide project? Because your caring ministry will have many more opportunities for ministry, more support from church staff, and more credibility in the eyes of your members and attenders if you become recognized as a ministry in your church. Although your efforts may begin with only a few caring individuals, ultimately your prayers and efforts can help your entire congregation to become more of a caring church. Remember Jesus' word to His disciples: "Love one another" (John 13:34). Applying this command within the fellowship and ministries of the local church is just as necessary today as it was when Jesus taught His disciples to love each other in the same way that He loved them. The watching world can observe the results of real discipleship when Christians demonstrate Christlike love to one another within local fellowships. As Jesus said, "All men will know that you are my disciples if you love one another" (John 13:35).

What Is a Church-Wide Project?

A church-wide project is one that will capture the imagination and provide an opportunity for the involvement of every member and attender in a caring project. No special qualifications, no training, no previous experience are necessary. *Anyone* can have a significant, satisfying part in such a project. Think in terms of doing projects which can involve as many members and attenders as possible.

Your ultimate goal with any church-wide venture is threefold:

1. *To meet a specific need* in a practical way
2. *To personally involve* as many members and attenders in the caring project as possible
3. *To establish the identity and purpose* of your caring ministry in the minds of your church staff, members, and attenders.

The size of the project you select may depend upon the size of your congregation. Small churches can easily organize a group of workers to do home repairs or remodeling. A larger church can tackle a refugee sponsorship, or even take complete responsibility for organizing, staffing, and running a soup kitchen. Any church, large or small, can do a food collection project for the benefit of needy members or to help stock a community food pantry. Your particular church's membership, location, resources, and your caring ministry team's vision will help you to select a suitable church-wide project.

When the plans for a church-wide project are initiated and carried out by lay people, that project will be more likely to succeed because it will have strong grassroots support. Church-wide projects do not need

to originate from the pulpit. They will be more effective
if they come from the people in the pews. The larger the
number of people involved, the better. A well-estab-
lished network of willing, available, enthusiastic volunteers will insure that one or two are not saddled with
complete responsibility for the success of the project. If
you can put together an experienced leadership team
(made up of individuals who have already demonstrated
their ability to lead and organize) you will prevent burn-
out for yourself and the others doing the planning. If
you are considering doing a church-wide project for the
first time, remember you will learn most by actually
doing the project. Pray, dream, plan, and act! Don't let a
previous lack of experience or shortage of personnel
stop you from attempting a church-wide project.

Surround your project with prayer, especially when
you are introducing such a plan for the first time in
your fellowship. Pray daily about your project. Pray for
the Holy Spirit's guidance and enabling in the selection
of leaders and recruiting of workers. Pray that your project will fire the imagination of everyone in your church.
Pray in detail for the organizational aspects, and pray
in faith for results that will glorify God. If your congregation meets regularly for prayer, or if you have a prayer
chain or prayer group, keep your prayer-warriors well-
informed. Getting people to pray regularly for the project will provide the confidence that comes from knowing you have prayed through all of the details. Sharing
prayer requests and updates will also help to keep everyone informed about the status of the project and reinforce other forms of communication about the project
to the congregation.

Avoid asking your pastoral staff to take any major
personal responsibility for any part of the proposed project. But do make sure that you consult with them regularly during the planning process. Invite a pastor to
attend at least one of your planning team's meetings if
at all possible. He will provide real encouragement to

your team, and often a pastor can offer advice that will enable you to carry out your project more effectively. Involve your pastor in the planning and communication processes, but do not expect him to do any of the major tasks in the project. His schedule is probably already bursting, and he will be delighted to know there are some volunteers he can count on to take the initiative in a ministry.

The pastor's endorsement of the project and his support for your ministry can best be communicated if he will announce the church-wide project to the congregation, or describe it in the church newsletter or bulletin. If your church board or leadership team needs to officially approve your plan, their support and approval can be communicated in the same ways. Do a thorough job of informing your church's staff and leaders, and keep in close contact with them throughout the project. Their encouragement, approval, counsel, and support will keep you going if you encounter difficulties, and their backing will make it easier for you to recruit people to help with every aspect of whatever project you tackle. Be sure to thank your staff and leaders for their help. Tell them often that you appreciate their support. If your church has an office staff or receptionist, make sure they are given a complete briefing on what any project involves. Give them your name and phone number and the names and numbers of others they can call for more information or answers to questions.

Four Action Steps

Four simple action steps will guide you through the process of planning, executing, and following-up on any church-wide project. If you'll follow the acronym POLE—*P*lan, *O*rganize, *L*ead, and *E*valuate, you'll have a simple planning method to guide your efforts. These four action steps will help you to think through and carry out any church-wide project effectively. Keep each of the four action steps in mind before, during, and after every church-wide project you attempt.

Plan your project carefully, then work your plan. Careful advance planning will help you communicate your vision for the specific project clearly, help you recruit many participants, and guide you through the project in an orderly manner. A clear plan will help you remember important details, especially when you are in the midst of doing the project. As you develop your plan of action for a church-wide project, write out a brief description of your plan. This will become a handy road map during your project, and it will be helpful later as a written record of what you attempted and accomplished.

Organize. Attention to detail as you organize a church-wide project is essential. Never assume anything. If you delegate a responsibility, follow through later to make sure the assignment was completed. Careful organization and easy-to-follow guidelines for every aspect of the project will increase your effectiveness as a project leader and manager.

Lead. Someone—a leader or a team of leaders— must take personal responsibility for each stage of a church-wide project. Leading calls for a blend of vision, prayer, patience, common sense, hard work, and a sense of humor. As the project leader or a member of a leadership team, remember that your enthusiasm, your personal commitment, and your example will have a direct impact on the effectiveness of your caring ministry's church-wide project. Spiritual leadership is not a position, title, or honor conferred on someone with the right connections. Spiritual leadership is a way of life. Effective, biblical leadership includes leading by *being* and leading by *doing.* A leader's life must be exemplary. He or she must set an example that others will follow. The best leaders lead by serving others, and the art of following is the first qualification for leading. Whether you are a leader or a follower, be the best you can be, and do the best you can do for the Lord.

Evaluate. Evaluation comes after you've completed your church-wide project. Set aside an hour or two and meet with your project team to review your work. Ask yourselves evaluative questions, encourage frank discussion, and honestly share both strengths and weaknesses with a view to doing a little better on your next project. Ask questions such as: What were the results of our church-wide project? How would we change our approach next time? What mistakes did we make? How could we correct them next time? What did we learn from this project?

As well as probing general successes and failures, encourage each team member to jot down personal lessons and observations. Then make a list of key points mentioned during the evaluation session. Keep a written record of your evaluation for future reference. Assign someone the responsibility of writing up the results of your project for your church newsletter or bulletin. Occasionally, you may decide to share a report on a church-wide project with your denomination's magazine or with a local newspaper.

Planning, Organizing, Leading and Evaluating are four action steps that will help you and your team to do a church-wide project effectively. Remember to emphasize individual and small group participation at every stage of the project. Your goal is to *personally involve* as many of your members and attenders as practical. You will help create a sense of ownership if you follow the advice of Dr. James Yen, founder of the International Institute of Rural Reconstruction in the Philippines, who writes,

> Go to the people
> Live among them and learn from them.
> Work with them and plan with them.
> Build on what they have.
> Teach by showing and learn by doing.
> Not a showcase but a pattern, and not odds and

ends but a system.
Not relief, but release.
Start with what they know and build upon what
they have.
But of the best leaders,
When their task is accomplished and their work
is done,
The people all remark,
"We have done it ourselves."[1]

Many of the key principles for an effective church-wide project are included in the two projects described in this chapter. One, a brown bag food collection project, can be done by any church that is interested in doing a church-wide project. Two, sponsoring a refugee family, also illustrates how much a small group of people can accomplish when they coordinate a church-wide caring project. The first project was initiated by two individuals, the second was initiated by the elder board of my church when the board chairman asked our caring group if we would take responsibility for organizing the church's sponsorship of a refugee family. My own involvement in both projects has convinced me that doing a church-wide caring project is one of the most rewarding ministries you can ever be involved in. Try one soon!

Try a Brown Bag Project

One of the best projects for involving a complete congregation is a brown bag food drive. If your church already has a soup kitchen or food distribution program, or if your caring ministry is already working with a food pantry in your city or town, then a brown bag project is something many families and individuals can get excited about doing.

Before you plan a food drive, make sure you know what you will do with the food you collect. A call to another church which is already involved in such a ministry, or to a social service agency which collects and distributes food, should provide some alternatives if you don't already have a specific outlet of your own.

Start planning your brown bag project at least two months ahead of your food collection day. We did our first church-wide food collection on Thanksgiving. This is an ideal time to introduce such a project on a church-wide scale as many churches and church members will have done something similar at previous Thanksgivings, and various families may already have a tradition of giving food to the needy at that time of year.

Regardless of what you have done in the past, your objective in doing a brown bag project on a church-wide basis is to involve the whole church in a caring project. Request permission to schedule the project from your pastors, or your church board—whichever is necessary. Once food collection day is scheduled as part of a regular worship service, write up an announcement for your church newsletter or bulletins each week for two or three weeks before the actual food collection day. You should also arrange for your pastors to announce the project from the pulpit in the weeks preceding the collection. If your church has never done such a project before, allow more time and do extra publicity. Posters strategically placed around your church, and announcements in Sunday School classes will help to get the word out.

Next, arrange to collect enough grocery bags so you have one for every family unit or individual in your congregation. Most supermarkets will be happy to donate the bags you'll need if you explain what they will be used for.

Then provide a menu/shopping list to be stapled to each grocery bag. This should list enough nonperishable food items to feed a family of four for three days. The brown bags with the menus attached should be passed out during the morning service the week before the scheduled food collection day. Or, you may decide to pass out just the menu/shopping list several weeks ahead of time to give more lead time to those who might prefer to set aside food items from several trips to the store rather than doing all of the shopping for the project at one time. Here's a sample list of nonperishable foods which will serve a family of four for three days:

Vegetables—three 16 oz. cans
Fruit—four 16 oz. cans
Noodles—one package
Cereal—one large package
Peanut butter—one 18 oz. jar
Soup—three 10¾-oz. cans
Macaroni and cheese—one package
Fruit juice—one 48 oz. can or jar
Meat (tuna/chili)—three cans
Crackers—one box
Powdered milk—one small package
Jello—two boxes

A bag of groceries like this will cost between $15 and $25 depending on the brands selected. Encourage families to include children in the shopping so everyone in the family understands and participates in the project. Some families may want to set aside money from personal allowances to buy the food, some will want to give out of their food budget, and others will decide to make their brown bag an extra gift—over and above their normal giving and routine family expenses.

Be prepared for those who may want to give a large cash gift for the purchase of food instead. Some may prefer to do that to enable a food pantry, the church, or a community agency to buy in bulk at substantial savings. Those who want to should be encouraged to give in that way. Remind them, and any others who may ask, that the value of a brown bag project is giving everyone an opportunity for personal involvement in a ministry to hungry people. After taking part in a brown bag project, some members of your church may be more interested in assisting regularly at a food pantry than they would have been previously. Others may be able to donate food in bulk if they own a restaurant or store, or if they work in a large food warehouse. Be prepared to arrange for the pickup of such donations. Within a week or two of completing our first brown bag project, I was contacted by one member of our church who had a freezer he was willing to give to anyone who could use it. We quickly arranged for the freezer to be installed at a cooperative church pantry in our area which had needed a freezer for some time.

Some churches who do a brown bag project may want to plan an entire worship service around their food drive. Hymns can be chosen to emphasize God's blessings and the believer's responsibility to share with others. The Scripture readings and prayers can reflect the theme of sharing as well. The sermon can also be planned around biblical teachings on generosity, service, and ministry to the poor. During the worship service on food collection day, make sure that someone explains to your congregation what will be done with the food, who will receive it, and how those who know about needy families can arrange for them to receive some of the groceries.

Arrange to have a drop-off place *inside* the church sanctuary, if possible, so that families can place their gifts on a table or in an area set aside for the collection either before or during the service. You'll be thrilled to watch children helping their parents carry in their family's gift of groceries. Your excitement will grow as you watch the bags pile up. You'll praise God for your church members' generosity, and you'll thank Him for a project which inspires so many to become personally involved.

In one Sunday we collected over 250 bags of groceries—enough to fill a three-quarter ton van which delivered the groceries to a cooperative church pantry in our area. Approximately thirty bags were kept at our church so our pastoral staff would have a supply on hand for distribution to needy church members or others needing food. Another fifteen bags or so were personally delivered to needy families who live close to our church. And after filling one pantry's available storage space with bags full of groceries, some more food was delivered to another pantry in the community—it too was low on food.

While the practical results were encouraging to everyone, the personal results were even more encouraging. Conservatively speaking, one food collection project meant that our members and attenders gave an extra $2,500 to $3,000 in one week. Over 200 needy families received the food through the various pantries. And a whole church was encouraged to see what God did when the people were given an opportunity to share with needy families in the local community.

All it took was a small group of individuals to pray, plan, and organize the whole effort. Several months later, while evaluating the year's ministry, our pastors and elders listed the brown bag project as one of the most encouraging accomplishments of the year. Try a brown bag project if you want to encourage your church to reach out and bless needy people in your community. All it takes is one person, like you, to introduce such a project into the life of your church.

For us, one well-planned project which involved most of the families in our church revealed great generosity and illustrated how much can be done by a local church which cares and reaches out. Now we are thinking of ways to collect food year-round so the pantry we assist will not be without food at any time of the year.

Because our church is one of many providing food for a cooperative pantry, we do not have complete responsibility for stocking that pantry. Several churches enlist the volunteers who staff the pantry. Just as a church-wide project will be more effective when many individuals are involved, so a cooperative church project works more smoothly and is more easily managed when many churches are involved.

By making a brown bag project a church-wide project, you will also pave the way for personally involving some of your members in serving food to needy families through the pantries or soup kitchens you work with. If you approach every church-wide project as an educational opportunity as well as a practical project, you will multiply the results. Strive to introduce new ways of thinking and acting with each church-wide project you attempt. Try to foster an awareness of hunger locally, nationally, and worldwide.

Invite the staff workers from local food pantries, community service agencies, or national organizations, like Bread for the World, to speak to your congregation. Distribute helpful literature and encourage your church members to become active in the fight against hunger.

No one—no family, no needy individual—should go hungry in any North American community today. And our churches should be in the forefront of the crusade to prevent waste and to provide nutritious meals to all those who cannot support themselves. Encourage your church to reach out into the needy community for Christ's sake. Combine your words of faith with practical works of love and service to the hungry. Reach out, show the world you care, do something beautiful for God in and through your local church.

Sponsor a Refugee Family

I'll never forget the day when Bob, the chairman of our elder board, asked me, "Bern, would the Barnabas Group be interested in taking on the church's refugee project?" I was excited because this meant our church leadership viewed our caring ministry as an important part of the ministry resources in our church. Nevertheless, I still told Bob I would have to check with the other group members before agreeing to take on the project.

I'm glad we had already established the guideline,

*Unless we have people willing to do the project, we
will not automatically take on a ministry.* Whenever
you plan a church-wide project for your caring ministry, make sure you have the people resources you'll need
to execute the project effectively. Although some families and individuals have sponsored refugees single-
handedly, the complexities of sponsoring a refugee family can be handled more easily if you have an
enthusiastic, committed, and caring team of co-workers.

After discussing Bob's request with some of the
Barnabas Group members, several of us arranged a
short after-church meeting one Sunday morning so
other church members could learn how they could be
involved. During the first meeting, we were delighted to
learn that Mai (who was born and raised in Vietnam)
was willing to volunteer her time and services as an
interpreter and advisor on cultural matters. A doctor's
wife with four daughters, Mai was already deeply
involved with the local Vietnamese community. Yet she
still gave her time generously. Although we did not
know it when we met for our first meeting, we only had
a couple of weeks to complete all of the necessary preparations. Almost as soon as we had done the paperwork,
a family of six was on their way from a refugee camp in
the Philippines to Colorado Springs.

We soon had a committee of twelve making preparations to welcome our family. Bob, a pharmacist, offered
to look for an apartment or house for the family. After
many hours of searching for the right living situation,
Bob found an adequate house that could be rented by
the church for a reasonable amount.

Once we knew all of the available details on the ages
of the various family members, we presented the need
for furniture, appliances, clothing, bedding, and
kitchen supplies to the church. As I read the lengthy list
of items to the congregation one Sunday morning, I
wondered how people would respond. I was staggered

by the response—every item on the list was donated by someone in the church! Several men volunteered to help move the heavier appliances into the house, and others offered their pickups to collect the donations and deliver them to the home. In some cases, we had a choice between items. Multiple offers of washing machines, dryers, and beds were made within minutes of the close of the service. Throughout the following week, calls continued to come into the church or group members' homes offering a rice cooker, a vacuum cleaner, and numerous items of clothing. Al and Lana, who own and operate a tree nursery, offered to employ all the family members who were able to work. A group of women spent hours cleaning, stocking the kitchen, making beds, and trying to make the home as comfortable as possible. Two doctors offered to give medical checkups. And people from every walk of life had an opportunity to become personally involved with our refugee family.

The whole process was made easier by the commitment and involvement of our church board. After receiving several requests and inquiries from church members who wanted to see the church sponsor a refugee family, the board decided to support the project. Funds were set aside for the family so that rent, groceries and other essential expenses were covered.

Our refugee sponsorship was an appealing challenge to tackle as a church-wide project. Although only a few of us tried to learn the Vietnamese pronunciation of the family members' names, everyone in the church thought of the Huynh family as "our" refugee family.

Five weeks after we greeted this family at the Colorado Springs airport they decided to move to Denver to live with some relatives. Because their decision to move came suddenly and unexpectedly, we struggled to decide if we had succeeded or failed in our first refugee sponsorship. Yet our post-sponsorship evaluation gave us an opportunity to learn some lessons which will help us if we decide to sponsor another refugee family in the future.

Whatever church-wide project you select, keep the following principles in mind while planning and carrying out the project:

1. Select an imaginative, challenging project.

2. Involve as many people as possible.

3. Lay men and women should initiate and carry out the project.

4. Integrate your caring ministry as one of the many ministries of your local church by doing a *church-wide* project.

5. Surround your ministry with prayer.

6. Consult with your pastoral staff and other church leadership throughout your project—keep them well-informed.

7. Plan, Organize, Lead, and Evaluate—POLE.

8. Make sure you have enough committed people to do the project you have selected.

For Study or Discussion

1. According to the author why should you do a church-wide project?

2. Discuss or list some possible projects you could do church-wide.

3. What does POLE mean? Discuss each action step.

4. Using the eight principles listed at the end of the chapter as a checklist, evaluate some of your selected church-wide project ideas.

5. Read Acts 11:27-30. What ministry principles do you see in this passage? Make a list of key principles for future reference.

6. Select another passage of Scripture which includes helpful principles for effective ministry. Explain how you would apply those principles in a church-wide project.

Note
1. James Yen, as quoted by Bryant Myers in "For People by People—The Development Process," in *World Vision Magazine*, November, 1982, p. 13.

Chapter 6

Multiply Many Caring Ministries

One week after Bill's local church-based caring ministry resettled a Vietnamese refugee family, another church member asked Bill if he would help teach a series of English classes for several refugee families in the city. Politely, but firmly, Bill explained he could not personally help out. Although it may have seemed natural for Bill to keep on ministering to refugees, he had to face the question of priorities too. Instead of focusing all of his time and effort on just one area of ministry, Bill wanted to stimulate and multiply many different caring ministries in his local church.

If you begin a caring ministry in your local church, win the support of church leaders, and complete one church-wide project successfully, you will probably find yourself standing in Bill's shoes one day. If God uses you as a catalyst—a person who helps start new ministries in your local church—you need to know in advance how you will answer such a request for assistance. Decide now that you will not automatically say yes and assume the responsibility for leading or organizing every new ministry you help to start or which others ask you to organize. Encourage other church members to use their gifts in leadership roles. Follow the advice Paul gave Timothy: Look for reliable men and women whom God gifts and calls—individuals you can coach, encourage, and train to minister within your local church (see 2 Tim. 2:2).

Unfortunately, local churches often tend to look for professionals—suitably qualified, so-called "experts"—whenever a new ministry need is identified. Relying on professionals to do the ministry, rather than encouraging lay people to do the ministries God has gifted and called them to do within the church, severely limits the ministry potential of any church.

But the multiplication of many kinds of caring ministries within a church will help it to fulfill its ministry potential. So concentrate your time and effort on multiplying many different kinds of caring ministries in your local church.

As Tom Sine observes:

> It is past time for local churches to change their emphasis from hiring professional staff to challenging and equipping local people to be the church. One of the major priorities of both the church and small community structures in the eighties and nineties must be the motivating and equipping of the laity to use a much greater part of their lives in service to others.[1]

Encouraging and equipping lay people to do the ministry is a biblical strategy, one Paul outlined for the church at Ephesus when he urged the believers there to live lives worthy of God's calling. Paul explains to the Ephesians the way in which apostles, prophets, evangelists, and pastors and teachers are all expected to teach and train believers to become servants. The church's spiritual leaders are called "to prepare God's people for *works of service*" (Eph. 4:12, italics added). A local church ought to show a limitless variety of creative works of service. By multiplying many caring ministries, a local church can involve all of its members in practical opportunities to share their faith with others.

The biblical model for the local church as described by Paul in Ephesians, shows that the church's leaders must focus their efforts on training the members of the body to serve others. When this happens, spiritually mature Christians demonstrate their faith by doing many kinds of "works of service." As a result, the Holy Spirit builds up the whole Body of Christ. Each member of the Body must do his or her part. Individually, the church leaders carry out a pastoral and teaching ministry and provide guidance and counsel to those leading lay ministries, while the members of the Body apply what they learn in "works of service." Corporately, the whole Body is built up and grows in faith and unity. "Speaking the truth in love, we will in all things grow up into him who is the Head, that is, Christ. From him the whole body, joined and held together by every supporting ligament, grows and builds itself up in love, *as each part does its work*" (Eph. 4:15-16, italics added).

Explore Many Kinds of Ministry

The kinds of caring ministry which your church develops will depend on the vision and resources of your church, and the needs and opportunities within your community. You can expect the people who become involved in action-oriented caring ministries to be the kind of men and women who will initiate new ministries as God expands their vision. Their willingness to serve and take responsibility for new ministries will become one of your church's most valuable assets. As you work with gifted, visionary church members, encourage them to use their gifts in service to others. Don't hold them back; encourage them to explore many different kinds of ministries. It's better to learn by doing and failing than not learning anything simply because no one bothered to act. Encourage others to exercise their faith by caring for others. Regularly review the inventory of your members' talents and resources, and pray specifically that God will lead each person to use his or her resources as He reveals new opportunities to serve Him.

Often ministry needs within a local church will overlap with needs in the local community. Therefore, your caring ministry groups can be either primarily church-oriented or primarily community-oriented; or your caring ministries can work on projects that affect both church and community.

If you're wondering just how many different opportunities there are for specialized caring ministries in a local church, consider this list adapted from William Pinson's helpful book *Applying the Gospel:*[2]

Family Life
Adultery
Aging
Dating
Delinquency
Discipline in the home
Divorce
Family finances
Housing
Husband-wife relationships
Marriage
Marriage preparation
Mental illness
Parent-child relationships
Relationships with relatives
Sex education
Single parents
Working wives and mothers

Citizenship
Church-state relations
Civil disobedience
Conscientious objection
Corruption in government

Courts and legal reform
Crime and punishment
How to have political influence
Individual freedoms
Law, order, and justice
Military-industrial complex
Organized crime
Prison reform
Political action
Political education
Private schools
Public education
Public funding of private schools
Revolution
Taxation
Violence
Voter registration
Voting
War and peace

Race Relations
Busing
Discrimination in employment
Investment in minority financial institutions
Inferior health care for minorities
Open housing
Prejudice
Racism
Segregation

Economics
Abuse of credit
Advertising
Child labor
Consumer protection
Computers
Inflation
International trade

Job safety
Labor-management relations
Leisure
Migrant workers
Poverty
Technology
Underemployment
Vocational choice
Wage scales
Welfare programs
Working conditions

Special Moral Concerns
Abortion
Adequate medical care
Alcohol
Drug abuse
Euthanasia
Gambling
Honesty
Hunger
Mass media
Mental health
Nuclear weapons
Pollution
Population explosion
Pornography
Prostitution
Retardation
Sanitation
Sex abuse
Suicide prevention
Tobacco
Traffic safety
Venereal disease
Women's rights

As you consider such a detailed list you may discover

issues that especially concern members of your local church. Or you may prefer to develop your own list of concerns based on your knowledge of your church and current needs in your community.

Form Study/Action Groups

Local churches can encourage members to form study/action groups to research issues like these which are currently affecting their membership and/or their community. These study/action groups can explore a particular issue and report their findings to the church. Or, they can begin a new caring ministry to do something about a specific issue—either within the local church or in the community.

As the report on *Evangelism and Social Responsibility* from the 1982 international consultation on the relationship between evangelism and social responsibility explains:

> The church should encourage its members to become conscientious citizens, to take the initiative to found and operate social programmes, to inform themselves about political issues, and to advocate or dissent according to their consciences.
>
> Since individual action is usually limited in its effects however, Christians should also be encouraged to form or join groups and movements which concern themselves with specific needs in society, undertake research into social issues, and organize appropriate action. We welcome the existence and activity of such groups, for they supplement the church's work in many important areas. Christians should also be encouraged to participate responsibly in the political party of their choice, their labour union(s) or business association(s), and similar movements. Whenever possible, they should

form a Christian group within them, and/or
start or join a Christian party, union or movement in order to develop specifically Christian
policies.[3]

For many issues, national organizations, parachurch ministries, or community agencies do already
exist and are doing an excellent job. You can encourage
your church members to become active in those existing ministries and agencies whenever possible. Parachurch groups and other movements specialize in ways
that local churches cannot. Some local churches, therefore, may decide to support national organizations,
parachurch ministries, or existing local agencies with
both people and finances, instead of beginning a new
organization. Or, a local church might decide to form
its own study/action group and encourage individual
members to join the other organizations as well. Most of
them will have educational resources—from films to
newsletters—that your local church can use. Again, the
decision to form your own ministry or study/action
group for meeting a specific need should be based upon
your local church's resources, current needs in your
community, and the ways in which the Holy Spirit is
leading your church's leaders and members.

Educate, Act, and Evaluate
The process of multiplying small-group caring ministries will always include the need to educate, act, and
evaluate. As a lay person, one of your most important
roles will be educating other lay people to develop biblical convictions and motivate them to act out their convictions in both the church and the local community.
The best way to stimulate others to act is to set them a
personal example—act out your own convictions. As
you do, others will learn and follow your lead. Regular
evaluation will help you determine the effectiveness of
your caring ministry and suggest improvements and

changes that need to be made. At each stage of the process of forming small-group caring ministries, try to involve as many lay people as possible. Build your ministry on the lay members of your church, and invite pastoral staff to help motivate, encourage, and train your key team members. Facilitate the multiplication of new ministries by sharing the experience gained from existing caring ministries. Reviewing the need to educate others, possible action steps to take, how to write a ministry plan and how to evaluate a potential ministry will sometimes stimulate the formation of new caring ministries to meet specific needs.

William Pinson outlines the four essential steps in the education phase:[4]

1. Stimulate concern.
2. Overcome resistance.
3. Establish guidelines.
4. Develop organization.

Then he gives seven specific steps for social action:[5]

1. Identify problems (or look for opportunities).
2. Locate resources.
3. Evaluate methods of social change.
4. Determine priorities.
5. Plan for specific action.
6. Act.
7. Review and revise.

These are helpful guidelines, though in practice many will want to act first and then develop plans and procedures based on experience. Those who prefer systematic, clearly organized procedures will be able to follow Pinson's suggested steps more closely. Whichever method you follow—whether you act first, or plan carefully before acting—your ministry team must decide what opportunities, needs, or problems you will get involved with. Deciding priorities and choosing where to invest your people, time, and money must be reviewed carefully and often. Analyzing your priorities prayerfully will help you decide which kinds of ministry your church should begin, or which kinds of extra ministries you should consider starting. William Pinson suggests five key questions to help you determine your ministry priorities:[6]

1. Which social problems affect most people in our community?
2. Which problems are the most seriously damaging to human life?
3. Which needs are being dealt with in the least adequate way by other groups?
4. Which problems are we best equipped to handle in the light of our resources?
5. Which needs do we feel God is leading us to deal with?

Write Out a Ministry Plan

After considering ministry priorities, write out a ministry plan. Briefly describe your ministry objective. State what you plan to do and how you plan to do it. Then list the specific action steps you'll take to accomplish your ministry objective. Recruit and motivate the people needed to get the job done. Build into your ministry a plan for training new leaders. Teach your leaders how to train others to do the ministry. Assign specific responsibilities, and suggest a timetable for each action step in your ministry plan. Then act! Prayerfully carry out your ministry plan, trusting God for His blessing and lasting results. Review, evaluate, and revise your plan as needed.

Evaluate Carefully

As you evaluate your progress, consider the following review questions from *Applying the Gospel:*[7]

1. Are we achieving the goal we set out to reach?
2. If not, why not?
3. What unforeseen obstacles or difficulties have come up?
4. How can we overcome them?

5. What mistakes have we made?
6. How can we profit from them?
7. Is the ministry worth continuing?

Whether you are just starting a caring ministry, or already have several different kinds of caring ministries underway in your church, effective leadership and clear communication will help you to keep on track and multiply your ministry.

Share Your Leadership

As you begin meeting needs and multiplying the kinds of caring ministries your church attempts, do not attempt to control everyone or everything that happens. Perhaps God will use you to start a particular ministry but then use others to carry on that work. Step aside graciously, and encourage the new leaders.

Remember, too, that every good leader trains his or her replacement. Pray that God will raise up your replacement as soon as you begin a new ministry. Strive to be an excellent team player. Do not dominate your caring ministry team. Do not dictate what the team can or cannot do. Share your vision, share the work, and share the leadership of the ministry with others.

If you regularly practice encouraging others to meet needs, serve, and lead, you'll do yourself a favor, for no one enjoys working with the kind of leader who must personally make every decision, approve every plan, or get involved in the details of every project.

And if you can learn to lead by serving those you lead, you'll help your co-workers develop their leadership potential. Give others the opportunity to lead. Congratulate them when they succeed. Encourage them when the going gets tough. And pray together regularly for the Holy Spirit's direction and enabling.

You are "God's fellow workers" (2 Cor. 6:1), and each member of the team can make a valuable contribution. Glorify God by the way you lead your ministry. The results of your work are in His hands; both the failures and the successes belong to Him. "I am the Lord; that is my name! I will not give my glory to another" (Isa. 42:8).

By sharing your leadership in this way you'll learn to trust the new leaders who are learning by watching how you lead. And learning to share your leadership will enable you to help multiply the many different kinds of ministries that can flourish in your church.

Communicate Clearly

The more ministries there are in a local church, the more crucial the communication process becomes. As the leader of a caring ministry you must learn how to communicate clearly and effectively.

Share your vision and your plans regularly with your church's staff and the church council or board. Keep your team members regularly informed about needs, opportunities, decisions, and projects. Let other ministry leaders know your caring ministry's goals, plans, and needs. Use church bulletin boards, newsletters, Sunday School teachers, and announcements from the pulpit to share what you are doing with as many members of the church as possible.

Clear, regular communication will encourage your church members when they hear what your ministry team is accomplishing. Clear communications will also help you to recruit new team members and make known specific needs for material and financial resources.

Clear communications will integrate your ministry or ministries into the total life and ministry of your local church. So communicate clearly. Let the local Body see and hear what your specialized ministry arm is up to. And when you start multiplying caring ministries, clear communications will help you explain why the new ministries are needed and how they will relate to one another. By modeling the art of communicating clearly, you will help the new ministry leaders see one of the key skills they'll need in their work also.

Ultimately, God raises up and multiplies new ministries in the local church. The Holy Spirit works in an individual's life, and soon the congregation can see and hear how God is blessing others through that person's ministry. Then a small group of like-minded individuals begins meeting regularly to pray, study the Bible, and discuss current issues. A new caring ministry is born as a group of concerned Christians start demonstrating God's love to others in and through their lives and service.

The lay leader's attitude is one key to the multiplication of many ministries—he or she must be willing to train others to lead also, and be eager to give them actual experience in leading. And the various ministry principles included in this chapter will also help you multiply many different kinds of caring ministries in your local church.

To summarize:

1. Use a biblical strategy to train the laity to do the ministry.
2. Explore and encourage the development of many caring ministries.
3. Form study/action groups.
4. Educate, act, and evaluate.
5. Use non-church resources (parachurch groups, community agencies).
6. Write out a ministry plan.
7. Share your leadership.
8. Communicate clearly.

Remember Bill? He's the caring ministry leader mentioned at the beginning of this chapter. He chose wisely, because the English classes for refugees which he was asked to teach have since become another church member's successful ministry. And Bill was left free to motivate other potential ministry leaders and to help start new caring ministries in other areas of need in the local church.

Because the opportunities for caring are so vast, there's no limit to what God might do through lay-led, Spirit-directed caring ministries in your local church. As lay persons who want to make a difference in our churches and in our world, let's join with Tom Sine, author of *The Mustard Seed Conspiracy*, in praying for the creativity needed to do all we can for God's glory:

> Let's invite the Holy Spirit to flood our imaginations and help us create innovative new ways to more effectively use our lives, our resources, and the underutilized resources of our churches for the service of others.[8]

For Study or Discussion

1. Look at the ministries list adapted from *Applying the Gospel*. Check those that apply to your church that offer opportunities as a group ministry. Use William Pinson's "five key questions to help you determine your ministry priorities."

2. What other concerns can you think of?

3. Select one concern. Read William Pinson's "four essential steps in the education phase" and brainstorm or list ways you can make the church aware of this concern.

4. Think about all of the existing ministries in your local church. Select one you would like to encourage, and then write out a practical action plan of how you would do that. Then do it!

5. In your opinion, what are some of the keys for multiplying *many* caring ministries in a local church?

6. Discuss your ideas for multiplying caring ministries with at least one other person in your church. If possible, discuss your concerns with a study group or Sunday School class.

Notes
1. Tom Sine, *The Mustard Seed Conspiracy*, (Waco, TX: Word Books, 1981), p. 177.
2. William M. Pinson, *Applying the Gospel*, Suggestions for Christian Social Action in a Local Church, (Nashville: Broadman Press, 1975), pp. 68-71.
3. Lausanne Occasional Papers No. 21—Grand Rapids Report—*Evangelism and Social Responsibility an Evangelical Commitment* (Lausanne Committee for World Evangelization and the World Evangelical Fellowship, 1982), p. 47.
4. Pinson, *Applying the Gospel*, p. 40.
5. Ibid., p. 68.
6. Ibid., p. 82.
7. Ibid., p. 87.
8. Sine, *The Mustard Seed Conspiracy*, p. 178.

Chapter 7

Get to Know Your Neighborhood

A young man surrounded by an exuberantly joyful crowd walked purposefully down a country road. As the travelers neared two small villages, they caught sight of their destination and stopped to admire the view. Jerusalem—a bustling city, spread out below them. Most of the group drank in the breathtaking sight of the city of David in silence. But Jesus wept.

He wept over the city because its people had not welcomed Him as their Messiah. He wept over Jerusalem because He foresaw the city's imminent destruction at the hands of invading Romans. Jesus wept because He longed to have a personal ministry among the city's residents. Sadly, He explained that the people of Jerusalem had failed to recognize God's presence among them:

> If you, even you, had only known on this day what would bring you peace—but now it is hidden from your eyes. The days will come upon you when your enemies will build an embankment against you and encircle you and hem you in on every side . . . . They will not leave one stone on another, because you did not recognize

the time of God's coming to you (Luke 19:42-44).

Jesus also expressed His great love for Jerusalem on another occasion during a teaching visit to the city's Temple. "O Jerusalem, Jerusalem, you who kill the prophets and stone those sent to you, how often I have longed to gather your children together, as a hen gathers her chicks under her wings, but you were not willing" (Matt. 23:37).

Jesus loved this city dearly, and wanted to share God's love with its people. He had a vision for this particular city, and after His death and resurrection Jerusalem became the birthplace of the Christian church.

Yet, even though He especially loved Jerusalem, Jesus had a similar vision for the many other villages, towns, and cities of His day. His twofold mission included proclaiming the gospel of the kingdom, and personally ministering to the physical and social needs of the people. Although a cosmopolitan, urbanized city like Jerusalem would eventually play a key strategic role in His global mission, Jesus did not neglect the small villages of Galilee (see Mark 1:38-39). Throughout His disciple-making ministry, Jesus thought globally and acted locally. He met the people of His day and ministered to them personally in their homes, neighborhoods, villages, towns, and cities. As Matthew observes, "Jesus went through all the towns and villages, teaching in their synagogues, preaching the good news of the kingdom and healing every disease and sickness" (Matt. 9:35).

As they traveled with Him, His disciples learned how to relate to spiritually and physically needy people right where they lived. Jesus did not remove His disciples from the needy world, He led them through it. After He entrusted the apostles with the responsibility of leading local congregations, they, too, followed His example and met individual physical and material needs on the local level—without losing sight of their ultimate goal, spreading the good news of salvation to all the world's unreached peoples.

Since Jesus combined local action with His world-wide mission, so must we. Lay persons and local churches must recover a vision that links a challenging global concern with concrete local actions. Like Jesus, we must love the people of our own neighborhoods and live among them as salt and light. We must get to know our local situation. We must familiarize ourselves with the people and the problems of our village, town, or city. Then we must expand our ministry horizons by sharing ourselves, and our faith, in service to the surrounding communities, our nation—even the whole world—as we follow the biblical pattern Jesus gave His disciples: "But you will receive power when the Holy Spirit comes on you; and you will be my witnesses in Jerusalem, and in all Judea and Samaria, and to the ends of the earth" (Acts 1:8).

Begin where you are, do what you can in your local setting, then trust God to lead you out into a world-changing ministry. Learn to think globally and act locally.

Individuals, families, small study/action groups, and local churches all need to get to know their neighborhoods and the contemporary world around them. As Dr. George Peters, professor of missions at Dallas Theological Seminary, writes:

> Christianity must focus on the world, live in the world, and serve in the world. It may not be easy but it is absolutely essential that a church that desires to be acceptable to the Lord, and experience the fullness of His blessings, that church must become a community of quality and quantity and be focused on the world. Only thus does its focus merge with the focus of God, and assure spiritual prosperity and progress in the

world. The world focus of the church is important—all important—for God so loved the world
. . .[1]

How do you begin to focus on living in and serving
the world? Think for a moment about people and
places. *Whom* do you live and work among? *Where* do
you live and work?

Answering these basic questions will immediately
show you, as an individual, some of the people God
wants you to serve. You will also identify one or two
places in which you, individually, can serve others. In
today's world it's common for someone to live in one
place and work in another. Similarly, most people today
interact regularly with several different groups of people. Christians today have multiple "neighborhoods"
and multiple neighborly-relationships.

Yet, because of the ever-increasing complexity of
modern life, the rapid pace of change, and the difficulty
of building lasting and meaningful relationships, it's all
too easy to look for impersonal ways to serve. It's easier
to write a check than it is to spend two hours helping
someone in need. There's also the tendency to become
involved in issues and causes without applying one's
beliefs on the everyday level. Once again, we must follow
Jesus' example. He went about doing good (Acts 10:38).
He practiced what He preached. Instead of giving a legal
expert a satisfactory definition of the word *neighbor*, for
example, Jesus described neighbor-love in action with
the parable of the Good Samaritan. Then He challenged
the lawyer to *"go and do likewise"* (Luke 10:37). Jesus
put His faith into action, and He challenged others to
do the same.

Every member of a local church should also have a
special concern for another significant neighborhood—
the neighborhood surrounding the local church. What
particular needs do the people who live near your
church have? How can your local church have an

impact in its immediate neighborhood?

Concerned Christians will want to pray for the people who live around their church, get to know them, and learn how to serve them. And they will do the same for those living in the neighborhoods surrounding their homes as well.

At both the individual level and the local church level, simple personal observation and contacts with the residents of your various neighborhoods will supply many opportunities for creative caring. Walk around your block. Drive through your church's neighborhood. Pray for ministry opportunities. Visit with some of your neighbors in their homes and ask them how your local church could help them. Listen to their interests and prayerfully look for ways to meet their needs.

With thousands of people moving nationwide from city to city every day, it's easy to think of the traditional neighborhood as a relic from the past. But even in the most rapidly growing metropolises of the modern world, neighborhoods—clusters of people whose lives are intimately connected with one another—still exist. And local churches, small action groups, Christian businesses, and individuals are all finding creative ways to minister in and serve their neighborhoods.

For example, one local church in Mendenhall, Mississippi launched a new ministry to specific neighborhoods by commissioning two of its members for a neighborhood outreach in Jackson, Mississippi. John Perkins, founder of Voice of Calvary Ministries, describes this vision for reaching neighborhoods in *With Justice for All.* Although this particular ministry focused on a specific strategy—the 3 Rs: Relocation, Reconciliation, and Redistribution—its goal was to "faithfully be the people of God in our neighborhood" and that's a goal any local church can apply. Several of the other practical principles that characterized the Voice of Calvary's new neighborhood outreach in Jackson can also be adapted by churches who want to reach out in their neighborhoods. The main principles were:

1. *The sending church had a clear vision for a neighborhood ministry.* In John Perkins' words, they had a vision to "carve out of the heart of Jackson, Mississippi a community of believers reconciled to God and to each other—that was our dream. To bring together a fellowship of blacks and whites, rich and poor, who would live together, worship together, and reach out together as the people of God. We believed that if we would faithfully be the people of God in our neighborhood we could make a positive difference in the lives of people enslaved by poverty and racism."[2]

2. *The mission church in Jackson built its outreach to the neighborhood on a mutual ministry to each other.* "We could not truly operate as a Body unless we used our spiritual gifts to minister to each other . . . . And then we would have to blend our gifts together in reaching out into the neighborhood in a way that would meet the needs of people and bring glory to Christ."[3]

3. *The mission church selected a specific target neighborhood to minister in.* "We chose a target neighborhood which was about 80 percent white, and turning black. At the rate it was changing over, it would be all black in four or five years . . . . One of our goals was to transform the neighborhood into one where blacks and whites would live together in harmony."[4]

4. *Key ministry team members relocated themselves and their families in the neighborhood.* "We outlined a geographical area of a six-block radius within which the families in our community would live. Vera Mae and I moved from our house in another part of Jackson and bought a house in our ministry area. We knew that to be effective we had to live among the people we were ministering to."[5]

5. *When Christians from other neighborhoods were drawn to the new neighborhood church, they were challenged to help renew the churches in their own*

neighborhoods. "I encouraged everyone who did not live in our target community to join churches in their own neighborhoods. We were convinced that people who did not live in the target area could not really bear the burden of those who did. They would not have the same kind of concern for the target community as those who lived there and whose children went to school there. Several of these families, then, moved into our community. Some, of course, stayed where they were and found churches in their own neighborhoods. This decision, I believe, was crucial to our effectiveness in the neighborhood."[6]

These five principles will help other local churches to have similarly effective ministries.

The neighborhood ministry in Jackson also benefited from several other wise decisions. The new outreach included both a church and a parachurch ministry. The church nurtured the people's spiritual lives, while the parachurch organization initiated community development projects. The purchase of a large house seven blocks from Jackson State University facilitated a ministry to black college students. And the house also provided a convenient meeting place for Bible classes, which paved the way for a regular church fellowship. The community development organization buys old houses, remodels them and then sells them at reasonable rates. The church members belong to household groups which meet weekly for Bible study and sharing.

"Ideally we wanted these household groups to consist of people from the same neighborhood who would get to know each other by eating and playing and studying and praying together," writes Perkins. "This shared life, then, would strengthen their witness in their neighborhoods."[7]

Although some neighborhoods are easily identified, others are more difficult to pinpoint. If your church is located in a large urban area and you are thinking about selecting a neighborhood to minister in, you may first need to learn how to identify a distinct neighborhood within your city. In *Studying Your Community*, Roland L. Warren suggests some of the most common characteristics which help determine the boundaries of an urban neighborhood:

1. Look for natural or artificial boundaries such as rivers, roads, railroads, hills, and parks.
2. Neighborhood associations which have already defined their boundaries may help you pinpoint specific neighborhoods.
3. Neighborhoods are often characterized by a local area of trade stores and other clustered groupings of small businesses.
4. The neighborhood is often thought of as the area served by an elementary school, and the larger community or district as the area served by a high school.
5. Neighborhoods are often characterized by "the same type of people" who have many common activities and interests.
6. Census tracts and block statistics may help define a neighborhood.
7. Remember, too, that some neighborhood boundaries overlap.[8]

A Christian Business and the Neighborhood

Christian business people can also help to bring new life to their neighborhoods. As Tom Sine reports in *The Mustard Seed Conspiracy*, Stanley Hallett, a Christian urban planner, dreamed of ways to improve a South Side Chicago community with the help of local churches and community organizations who would work for justice for the people. In the 1950s the South Shore was an affluent, middle-class, white community. In time the white community fled to the suburbs, taking their business with them. South Shore became 85 percent black.

As Tom Sine explains, "The South Shore Bank dramatically cut back its service and the availability of financial resources to the community in 1972. This type of racist bank policy, called 'redlining,' paralyzes mostly poor, predominantly black or Hispanic communities."[9]

Ater a year's study, Stanley Hallett and some friends concluded that the local bank was the critical factor in producing either urban growth or decline. So they began raising money and acquired the South Shore Bank for $1.3 million in 1973.

They held meetings in churches and invited community residents to neighborhood coffees to learn what dreams the people had for their community. Hallett explained that the new bank owners deliberately focused on the capacities—the future potential—of the neighborhood, not its deficiencies. Hallett and others asked the residents questions like: "What is there to work with, what has the capacity to grow, to achieve? . . . We tried to figure out how we might create a self-sustaining neighborhood development institution. We didn't want one which would draw more and more resources, require more and more subsidies, and make more and more people dependent on next year's grant. We wanted one that would start to generate resources and would have a principle of growth instead of a principle of limitations."[10]

The bank clearly defined its commitment to the community's well-being. "While the policy of the corporation is to make loans and investments only in situations which it believes offer a reasonable expectation of return to the corporation, it will not attempt to maximize such return at the expense of its primary goal of developing the neighborhood for the benefit of its residents."[11]

As Tom Sine observes, a recent study concluded that "South Shore was indeed on the rebound. Property values were appreciating, the crime rate was down, median income had increased. Further deterioration was being prevented by active 'neighborhood organizations, increasing numbers of middle class blacks in the community and renewed commitments to the neighborhood by the South Shore Bank.' This Mustard Seed model of an innovative way to achieve economic justice is already being emulated in other communities."[12]

Christian business people can make a difference in local communities, especially if they are willing to follow such innovative and creative examples as this one. A host of men and women who will follow Stanley Hallett's example are needed. What would happen nationwide if every Christian business focused on the needs, dreams, and potential for growth in local neighborhoods? Yes, Christian businesses and business people can help to meet needs by providing job opportunities, resources, capital, and support for needy communities. This is a ministry opportunity that must not be overlooked. Every Christian business man or woman must prayerfully ask God to show him or her how a similar neighborhood project could be launched within his or her own business or sphere of influence in the business world.

The Wall Street Journal reports that some ninety large, national, food companies are donating their surplus food products to Second Harvest, a Phoenix-based network of fifty-seven city food banks which pass the contributions on to soup kitchens, pantries, and other emergency food outlets. And the companies report there has been an increase in the number of requests for their surplus food following the government cutbacks in food stamps, school lunches, and other feeding programs. One Chicago food bank, however, states that many smaller food companies are not aware of outlets for unsalable food.[13]

A Pastor Studies His Neighborhood

Pastors, too, can help local congregations get to

know their neighborhoods. While ministers are trained to explain the Word of God to their congregations, they also need to learn how to explain the contemporary world to their people. Pastors and lay people alike need to study current affairs, local, national, and global politics, and be able to relate to contemporary situations and needs from a biblical perspective.

Raymond Bakke is one of the founders of the Seminary Consortium for Urban Pastoral Education which provides urban training for seminary students. Formerly the pastor of Fairfield Avenue Baptist Church in Humboldt Park in inner city Chicago, Bakke now teaches urban ministry skills to students at Northern Baptist Theological Seminary. Bakke learned the importance of studying the urban world and developing an appropriate ministry during his own pastorate, and he now shares his insights with the pastors of tomorrow. "We need to teach pastors how to custom-build ministry; that is, how to move into a community, exegete the context, exegete the Scripture, and scratch where people itch," he said in an interview with *Leadership.*

In the course of his conversation with the editors of *Leadership,* Bakke shared some of the ways he personally learned about a church which had entered a period of decline. Although it was steeped in tradition and loyally supported by a core group of eleven members, the church's programs were no longer relevant to the neighborhood's needs. "Houses on the block were burning and the neighborhood was up for grabs," says Bakke. "I knew how to run programs. But if you're going to catch fish, you have to change bait and go where the fish are."

Going where the fish were meant getting to know the neighborhood in depth. As Bakke says, he began to "learn the language, listen to people talk, and begin to communicate Jesus with concepts people already understood."

The Fairfield Avenue church had a strong Swedish

heritage, but the neighborhood had become largely Spanish-speaking. Initially, the church members were unwilling to adapt, unwilling to get in step with the social changes surrounding their sanctuary. But their pastor persisted in his attempts to study his church, to relate to the church's neighborhood, and to initiate new ministries that would meet the needs of people living nearby. He carefully studied the history of his congregation, and personally discipled each new board member added over a five-year period. As the church's pastor, Bakke commended the church for their strong traditions. But he also challenged the membership to develop a forward-looking vision of their church's future ministry.

"The task of the preacher is remembering that until Christ comes, the past is a present memory and the future is a present possibility. In terms of practical pastoral work, this means taking the ethos of a group of people—the great memories and traditions of the church—and showing how they can be translated into present-day deeds that best serve the future," says Bakke.

Lay persons and pastors can learn much from the specific approaches that Bakke used in learning to know his inner city neighborhood. His simple, direct, personal approach is one anyone can learn from. He did three things: (1) He spent one day a week "networking"—visiting local pastors, community agencies and businesses to learn all he could about the neighborhood. (2) He asked his fellow pastors what they had learned about being pastors in the inner city. "Some of them took me by the hand and showed me the community—where kids hang out, where drugs get dropped, where things happen." Gradually, neighborhood people and problems came into focus. (3) He learned from the local police, and he learned from school principals. "The barber, the gas station attendant, the person who runs the fruit market—these people can tell you better than anyone what makes the neighborhood tick," says Bakke.

Like others ministering in the inner city, Pastor Bakke had his share of discouragements. But his approach motivated a declining church to multiply its outreach by helping start seven Spanish-speaking daughter churches in the neighborhood. "Our theory was that in a diverse neighborhood like ours, smaller, multiple churches were the way to go."

Learning to think small was the essence of Fairfield Church's ministry strategy. And Bakke encourages other pastors and congregations to think small in order to reach big cities. "Thinking small is a way of becoming more human. Bible studies, prayer circles, support groups, and service organizations are very important today. Rather than becoming single-issue preachers, we need to organize and minister to targeted groups of people doing specific tasks.

"A pastor can't meet all the needs in a church; a pastor can organize smaller special-interest groups to meet those needs. The way up for the church is to affirm a whole range of leadership styles and to allow smallness to create the intimacy where ministry can happen."

For Raymond Bakke, thinking small also meant learning not to expect success in terms of instant results or a big congregation. He learned to value the individual in his inner-city discipling ministry.

"I saw that if I reached a mother through her son, and five years later he married a Christian, I had broken the cycle of a non-Christian family. That delivered me from needing to see immediate gratification and large numbers. It enabled me to work with integrity with a person, knowing that just one person discipled is extremely significant."[14]

How a Layman Studied His Neighborhood

Just as pastors can help churches get to know their neighborhoods better, so can lay people. Dick Taylor, a lay member of the Jubilee Fellowship of Southwest Germantown, Philadelphia, was commissioned to study his neighborhood for his religious community. "Some of us don't even know our next-door neighbors, much less whether there's a lonely elderly person down the block," some members of the community said. "How can we talk about peace and social justice in the world if we aren't doing something about conflict, poverty, and injustice right around the corner?" others asked. So the group decided to ask Dick to do some research on their local community and report on his findings.

In an article he wrote on the project for *Sojourners*, Dick states that his research was based on the assumption that "as a loving parent God cares deeply about all our neighbors, and wants all his children to have what they need for their physical, intellectual, emotional, and spiritual well-being." He then set himself the task of finding out if there were any people in his neighborhood who were suffering, exploited, or in need. He wanted to discover who was hungry, out of work, or living in dilapidated housing. Dick began his research project with census data, then narrowed his efforts by reviewing readily available information from public and private agencies, neighborhood groups and individuals. As you soon learn from his report, he also learned by reading, contacting individuals and agencies, doing interviews and writing an eight-page report on his findings. The whole project took about twelve days.

United States Census data is compiled every ten years and published in books that can be found in most local libraries. When Dick examined the data for his neighborhood, he discovered there were about twelve thousand people living in fifty-nine hundred housing units.

> By looking at income and housing figures, I was able to pinpoint those sections of our neighborhood that are relatively well-off and those that

have severe poverty. I found the location of our good housing and our dilapidated, over-crowded housing. I also saw our unemployment rate and could compare it to the city's other areas. I learned that in the last 15 years a dramatic shift in the racial composition of Germantown had taken place as it went from a 97 per cent white community to one with a black population of more than 50 per cent.

While this kind of data is compiled once a decade, updates are available from the Census Bureau and other public and private agencies.

The area planners of Philadelphia's City Planning Commission supplied detailed maps showing every street, property, school, church, park and factory. The planners also gave Dick a briefing on city-sponsored plans for recreation, employment, housing, and industrial development in his neighborhood. By talking to the staff of the local Health and Welfare Council, Dick learned about local needs in recreational facilities, the problems of the young and the elderly, and many other social problems. He was given a directory of community services by the council as well.

"An appointment at one agency, the Northwest Center, gave me information on the people in our general area who suffer from such problems as mental disability and alcoholism. Conversations with staff at the Northwest Interfaith Movement told me how area churches are trying to respond to neighborhood needs."

To round out his research, Dick talked personally with staff and volunteers in the neighborhood and its local churches. "I spent considerable time simply walking and biking back and forth through the community, chatting with neighbors, shopkeepers, and others to get to know and feel the neighborhood."

In his final report to the Jubilee Fellowship, Dick described his findings in three categories—Human

Needs, Efforts to Meet Needs, and Possible Neighborhood Ministries for Jubilee Fellowship. The fellowship specifically wanted to consider possible new ministries in the light of four priority concerns:

1. A ministry to the poorest, those most in need, with no other advocate
2. A ministry that would provide a direct service, but have potential for social change
3. A ministry that would give the people ways to communicate their faith
4. A ministry that would better help us to understand our neighbors and their needs.

As a result of his efforts, Dick listed twenty-five ways his fellowship could meet these criteria for a neighborhood ministry. And there were personal benefits too. Dick writes:

> As I've become more deeply involved personally, I've made friends with an isolated 82-year-old man whose last close relatives died in 1917. During the last two bitterly cold winters, his tiny apartment was heated only by the burners of a dangerous gas stove. As we sit together in his little room, I sometimes feel I can say the words of one of Mother Teresa's workers in India: "I have been touching Christ; I knew it was him."[15]

Just as Jesus loved Jerusalem, so you can learn to love your neighborhood. Whether you are a pastor or a lay person, God has a special ministry for you in your local setting. Get to know your neighborhood by walking around it, or by biking or driving through it. Talk to your neighbors. Find out what their dreams are. Discover their personal needs and hurts. And pray. Pray for insight and wisdom about how you as an individual, how your small study/action group, and/or your local church can begin ministering to people in your neighborhood. If you want to help reach the world for Christ, begin right where you are—in your neighborhood.

For Study or Discussion

1. John Perkins' Voice of Calvary Ministry concentrates particularly on poor Southern black families. His 3 Rs are Relocation, Reconciliation, Redistribution. Discuss or write down how this plan would or would not work in your community.

2. Using a map of your city, town, or community, determine your church's ministry boundaries. What ministry opportunities are there within these boundaries? Are you effectively ministering to all areas within your church's area?

3. Think about your neighborhood for a moment, and list the people you would contact to get a better picture of the current needs and service opportunities where you live. What networks exist in your neighborhood? How can you learn from them?

4. Read the quotation from Dr. George Peters on page 137. Discuss his statement with the members of your study group, small group, or Sunday School class. How can Christians today develop a "world focus"?

5. Now consider the ways Jesus focused on the world during His earthly ministry. How can you personally follow His example? Be specific and write a brief paragraph explaining your answer.

Notes

1. George Peters, *A Theology of Church Growth* (Zondervan Publishing House, 1981), p. 253.

2. John Perkins, *With Justice for All* (Ventura, CA: Regal Books, 1982), p. 105.

3. Ibid., p. 106.

4. Ibid., p. 109.

5. Ibid., p. 110.

6. Ibid., p. 111.

7. Ibid., p. 111.

8. Roland L. Warren, *Studying Your Community* (New York: The Free Press, 1965).

9. Tom Sine, *The Mustard Seed Conspiracy* (Waco, TX: Word Books, 1981), p. 200.

10. Ibid., p. 200.

11. Ibid., p. 200.

12. Ibid., p. 201.

13. *The Wall Street Journal*, July 21, 1983, p. 1.

14. Raymond Bakke, as quoted in "No Church Is an Island," an Interview with Raymond Bakke," *Leadership*, Spring Quarter, 1982, pp. 111-120.

15. Dick Taylor, "Discovering Your Neighborhood's Needs," *Sojourners*, June, 1979, pp. 23-24.

Chapter 8

Cooperate with Other Churches

Apparently no denomination has a corner on the saints; they are about equally distributed among them. Apparently, God takes little or no cognizance of the denominational affiliation in the distribution of his grace and gifts. He gives his grace and gifts to those surrendered to and obedient to Jesus Christ without regard to labels. If you think God is not sufficiently observant of labels you had better take it up with him and take him to task. I am just reporting.[1]

As you cooperate with Christians from other denominations, you will make the very same discovery that E. Stanley Jones recorded in his spiritual autobiography, *A Song of Ascents*. Lay people who become involved in practical caring ministries have the delightful privilege of sharing their lives with, and learning from, Christians of all denominations. Protestants who become actively involved in social ministries soon discover that their Catholic brothers and sisters have often led the way in ministries of social responsibility.

As you start getting to know Christians from different denominations by working alongside them, you'll recognize that in the light of real human need, denominational distinctives and practices soon fade into the background of your concerns. You'll discover that your common faith in the Lord Jesus, and your common desire to serve the needy in His name, is a source of unity, joy, and strength.

Sherwood Eliot Wirt writes:

> The man of faith is outgrowing the temptation to turn his denominational haven into some kind of holy fort. Internecine warfare between believers who do not baptize, worship, or tithe in an identical mode is subsiding. Is Jesus Christ enthroned in a brother's heart? Does he measure his life by the God-inspired Scriptures of the Old and New Testaments?[2]

Wirt encourages his readers not to insist on pressing the agreement further. "The tie that binds," he adds, "is not ecclesiastical union, or uniformity of worship, or doctrinal niceness, but rather fellowship in the Beloved."[3] He goes on to suggest that "Christian social conscience should be as wide as the love of God in Christ," noting that "Jesus Christ preached to the multitudes, he had compassion on the multitudes, he died for the multitudes. As he was in the world, so also are we."[4]

Jesus also prayed for the unity of His followers. In John 17:20-23, we read:

> My prayer is not for them alone. I pray also for those who will believe in me through their message, that all of them may be one, Father, just as you are in me and I am in you. May they also be in us so that the world may believe that you have sent me. I have given them the glory that

you gave me, that they may be one as we are
one: I in them and you in me. May they be
brought to complete unity to let the world know
that you sent me and have loved them even as
you have loved me.

As you follow your Lord into a cooperative caring
ministry, you will experience a little of what Jesus had
in mind when He prayed that prayer. Doctrinal differ-
ences melt away, barriers to fellowship are removed,
and new co-laborers get to know each other when
Christians from many denominations resolve to work
together in Christ's name to minister to the poor and
needy. Every one who moves out into the real world of
hurting, struggling, despairing women and men dis-
covers needs far too big for any one church to handle on
her own. In the face of ever-growing social needs and
problems, we must work together—for Jesus' sake. He
will bless you richly as you discover the joys of cooperating with other Christians and other churches.

Practical Suggestions for Cooperation

The ever-growing need for social ministries in our
cities calls for inter-church cooperation. Because no
one church can solve this problem alone, cooperation is
not optional, but essential. If you research the need for
social services in your city or town, you will most likely
discover that the demand for those services already
exceeds the service agencies' capacity for meeting those
needs. Churches who become familiar with this need
must mobilize all of their resources—people, money,
and materials—and try to help meet those needs. This
cannot be simply a matter of individual churches acting
on their own, though some concrete action by a church
will be better than none at all. Rather, there must be a
willingness to cooperate with other churches and to
coordinate social ministries for the most effective quan-
tity and quality of service.

After researching local needs, the next step is to meet with key leaders from local churches in your area to discuss local needs, pray together, and share ways in which those needs can be met. A series of meetings between the churches interested in working together will usually be necessary to develop a satisfactory, well-thought-out plan of action.

Some churches will be able to build upon their congregation's existing outreach ministries, while others will need to develop new ministry teams and recruit and train new personnel. When you begin to explore the opportunities for cooperative ministry in your community, be sure that you review existing church ministries. Learn about what is already being done, define clearly what needs are not being met, and decide what your cooperative ministry's priorities will be.

When we formed Northern Churches Care in Colorado Springs, attendance at the initial meetings fluctuated between six and twelve churches. But gradually, in the course of a year or so, eight member churches continued to meet monthly and we established a new food pantry, a community resource bank of volunteers who are willing to donate their time and talents in service to others, and an emergency services center for interviewing and counseling the needy residents of our part of the city. (The emergency needs center provides some financial assistance, when finances permit, to those who are unable to pay their rent, mortgage, utility bill, medical expenses, or other emergency needs.) Though we are still in the process of establishing all of these services, we are working cooperatively with churches from several different denominations in our area to provide emergency assistance to people who have no other source of help. Churches and individuals support us financially—we began by asking member churches for $50 per month for emergency needs. But the majority of our services are donated, and we work exclusively with volunteers and have no paid staff.

Two churches donate the space needed for the food pantry and the emergency services interviewing office, and a member of one of our cooperating churches rents us a small apartment every month so we have a place to provide temporary emergency housing to families or individuals. Although our ministry is still in the beginning stages, we are encouraged by the amount of progress we've seen in just over a year of ministry. Currently, our members include Episcopal, Evangelical Covenant, Catholic, Conservative Baptist, and Methodist churches. Several churches of other denominations have worked with us occasionally, and we hope more will join us in the future.

Work Geographically

One reason we have been able to develop our cooperative network is that other churches in our city are taking some responsibility for their geographic area of the city. This means that no single group faces the prospect of serving all of the needy people in our city. By dividing Colorado Springs into Central, Northern, Southern, Western, and Eastern areas, we hope to provide some cooperative church ministries to supplement existing social service agencies throughout the city.

Most cities will have the potential to develop a similar network based on geography. If there isn't anything like this in your city or town, perhaps your church will help to pioneer a cooperative, inter-church ministry.

If you've already developed a caring ministry within your local church, think of a cooperative church ministry as an extension of your ministry into the community at large. Just as people are the most valuable resource in your caring ministry, so people will be the most valuable resource in your cooperative church ministry. Work at recruiting enough volunteers so no one gets overloaded. Share the leadership opportunities, and share the service opportunities. Ask many people to do a little at a time, instead of asking a few to do a lot of work all of the time.

As you begin ministering with other Christians from different denominations, you will naturally come into contact with the staff of various city, county, and federal agencies. And in the midst of these natural contacts you will have regular opportunities to demonstrate your faith and share the reality of God's love. Be willing to learn from any community volunteers and agency staff who have more training and experience than you, but be prepared to share your love and faith with them as you have opportunity.

Remember, social service ministries provide our churches with many opportunities to demonstrate the reality of our faith, the depth of our love, and the life-changing power of God in the midst of a hurting world. Churches must model a servant life-style to those in need and to the non-Christian professionals, agency staff, and volunteers who are working on behalf of needy people in the local community. What an exciting opportunity for every local church in North America! Local churches who reach out into the community with caring ministries will discover many new ways to share their faith at all levels of the community. Welfare agencies, social service departments, counseling clinics, medical centers, utility departments, and police departments will be pleased to see the churches of your community working together to serve those whom no one else cares for.

By helping to launch a cooperative church ministry in your area, Christians can also penetrate the social, business, and political leadership networks of your city or town. Christians must see the great potential that exists for making a life-changing impact locally. Social service ministries will provide many natural opportunities for witness—if we will take the initiative to work together.

Instead of waiting cozily in our churches for the people of our community to come to us, we must go out into the community and minister to them in their environment.

As Bruce Nicholls, executive secretary of the Theological Commission of the World Evangelical Fellowship, says, "Our mission must be motivated by the love of God and the example of Christ. We are called to leave our middle class ghettos and bear the marks of the Cross in the market place, the slums, the factories, and in the villages ministering to the poorest of the poor."[5]

Do you share Nicholls's vision? Are there bands of committed women and men and young people in your local church who will join hands with one another and team up with Christians from other local churches in your area to cooperate in ministries of social responsibility? If you have such a vision for a vigorous, cooperative outreach by many local churches, go to work today. Bring together those who share your vision and begin working together to help meet social and human needs in your area. Encourage your local churches to become known as worshiping, witnessing, and *serving* communities in your city or town.

What kinds of caring ministries are already underway in your local church? What specialized ministries are there in the other local churches in your community? How can the churches in your area cooperate more effectively in social ministries? Discuss these questions together, and act cooperatively. Broaden your local church's vision to include cooperative social ministries with the other churches in your area. As you begin working together, the churches of your community can make a community-wide impact. Start cooperating with some other churches in caring ministries today.

For Study or Discussion

1. List some other churches in your city and town that could be approached to cooperate in meeting more of your community's needs.

2. List the caring ministries already underway in your church.

3. Now list areas that still need attention and needs which your church is not meeting.

4. How will you approach other churches to cooperate in meeting these other needs?

5. Sherwood Eliot Wirt says, "The Christian social conscience should be as wide as the love of God in Christ." What are some specific ways in which a Christian can develop a more Christlike social conscience?

6. Read Bruce Nicholls's statement on page 159 again. Discuss your response with a friend, your study group, or a Sunday School class.

Notes
1. E. Stanley Jones, *A Song of Ascents* (Nashville: Abingdon Press, 1968), p. 289.
2. Sherwood Eliot Wirt, *The Social Conscience of the Evangelical* (New York: Harper and Row Publishers, 1968), pp. 6-7.
3. Ibid., p. 7.
4. Ibid., p. 8.
5. Bruce Nicholls, *Missionary News Service*, August 1, 1980, p. 2.

Chapter 9

Involve Your Church in Community-Wide Projects

The love of God cannot possibly be bottled up within the Christian community; it breaks out in compassion for the world. It yearns for the salvation of sinners, so that Christ's lost sheep may be gathered safely into His flock. It yearns also to alleviate the material needs of the poor, the hungry and the oppressed, so that if we close our hearts against the needy, we cannot claim that God's love abides in us (1 John 3:17). Love for God and love for neighbor belong inextricably together, as Jesus taught (Mark 12:28-34, compare 1 John 4:19-21).

We are convinced that the Christian impact on society (both evangelistic and social) depends even more on quality than on numbers, and the distinctive quality of Christians is love.[1]

Francis Schaeffer, a well-known author and teacher, calls love "the mark of a Christian."[2] And whether we consider the spiritual needs of unreached people, or the physical needs of the poor and hungry, Christian love demands an appropriate response. For too long we have debated the relationship between evangelism and social responsibility instead of encouraging local churches and Christians to do evangelism *and* ministries of social responsibility. Both kinds of ministry are urgently needed in today's world. Lay men and women can follow their Lord in both forms of ministry. And both evangelistic ministries and ministries of social responsibility should make an impact on society. Carrying lay people will encourage Christians to develop evangelistic, socially responsible, and loving life-styles—both individually and corporately. And we must begin at the local level by encouraging individual Christians and local congregations to become deeply involved in the local area through community-wide projects.

Community-wide projects will often result from cooperative church ministries. But some groups and organizations may be called into existence purposefully in order to stimulate the development of community-wide caring Christian ministries.

A Model for Community-Wide Service

One organization which exists to encourage and facilitate the development of caring ministries throughout the community is Evangelical Concern of Denver, Colorado. Evangelical Concern sees itself as a catalyst organization which attempts to establish new ministries designed to meet social needs. Evangelical Concern's statement of ministry explains this purpose:

> *Evangelical Concern provides encouragement and assistance.* Think of the function of a catalyst in any chemical equation. A catalyst triggers or speeds up a chemical reaction by being introduced into a substance, yet as a catalyst, it does not undergo any permanent chemical change in the process. On the contrary, it is usually recovered and used again.
>
> In the same way Evangelical Concern gives

impetus and assistance to people and organizations to help them react to society's social needs. Evangelical Concern educates, yet it does not usually become involved in the operation of the ministry itself.[3]

Evangelical Concern of Denver operates a resource center by maintaining relationships with national and local ministries, and by researching the need for social action. Evangelical Concern also seeks to educate others in the need for Christian social ministries. It does this by providing speakers to preach and teach in local churches, making study materials available, and providing resources for workshops, seminars, and conferences. And it sponsors an annual Social Awareness Conference to acquaint Christians with biblically-based local ministries in Denver, and to motivate them to become involved in those ministries.

To implement needed social ministries, Evangelical Concern will help form a task force to develop a ministry to meet a particular need. Task forces may be formed by individuals from one church or several. After a task force is established, Evangelical Concern serves the new ministry by helping to organize, research needs, raise money, and train volunteers.

Evangelical Concern's statement of purpose concludes with the following summary of their ministry:

> Confronted with the tremendous number of social problems in our age, Evangelical Concern is committed to encouraging evangelical Christians to become involved in meaningful ways to obey Christ's commands as revealed in Scripture, specifically the words of love (1 Corinthians 13), the fruit of the Spirit (Galatians 5:22-23) and the exemplary love of God shown to all men (Matthew 5:43-48).

In addition, Evangelical Concern is committed to reproducing itself in other communities. It attempts to interest Christians in other communities to start independent organizations with a similar commitment to social concern and justice.[4]

Information on the availability of workshops and presentations in communities outside Denver can be obtained by contacting Dr. Ron Bard, Evangelical Concern's Director, at 1230 Decatur Street, Denver, CO 80204.

The wide range of concerns and ministries currently being helped by Evangelical Concern and/or the organizations it aids include:

1. *Denver Habitat* assists low-income and poverty-level residents to purchase single family homes.
2. *The Native American Urban Transition Program* helps American Indians to survive the cultural transition from reservation to urbanization.
3. *Hope Communities* provides low-income housing assistance in the inner city.
4. *Ministry to the Handicapped* provides instructive manuals and support groups for the parents of handicapped children.
5. *Vietnamese Resettlement Program* helped to resettle eighty families in the Denver area.
6. *Parent Aide Ministry* helps support parents with Christian fellowship.
7. *Single Parents Ministry* ministers to single parents and their children.
8. *Tutoring Ministry* acts as a clearinghouse to help Christians become involved with tutoring inner-city children.
9. *Ministry to the Chronically Mentally Ill* recruits Christians to minister to displaced mentally ill on a one-to-one basis in Capitol Hill.
10. *F.R.I.E.N.D.S.* reaches out to the chronically mentally ill throughout Denver by means of social

clubs which provide gathering places for volunteers and stable clients.

11. *Bread for the World.* The original Colorado chapter of this international ministry was organized by Evangelical Concern. It participates in lobbying and advocacy efforts in the area of hunger and justice issues.

12. *COMPA Food Ministry* is a weekly food ministry that distributes food through fifteen evangelical churches and ministries. In 1982 and 1983, $200,000 worth of food was distributed at a cost of approximately $30,000.

13. *The Crisis Pregnancy Center* counsels pregnant women to help them avoid abortion.

14. *The Christian Conciliation Service* works to help promote resolution of disputes between Christians.

15. *Sunrise Ministries* is a ministry to the alcoholic and his/her family.

16. *The King's Ministries* is a Christian outreach to homosexuals.[5]

Through these ministries, Evangelical Concern of Denver is modeling a way that concerned, caring Christians can become involved in community-wide projects. And their model is one that other groups can follow in other communities. In many cities and towns a distinctively Christian organization that will serve as a catalyst to help establish social ministries is urgently needed.

"All it requires is faith and obedience," says Dr. Ron Bard, Evangelical Concern's third director. "You pray, plan, and step out. The process of obedience, 'the obedience that comes from faith' (Romans 1:5) is important. God will provide the resources, and He will take care of the results," says Ron.

When asking people to consider getting involved with social ministries Ron emphasizes the importance of doing something simple and attainable. Instead of asking someone to become involved in a program of social action, for example, he simply asks them to spend two hours a week helping people. He also encourages people to do what God encourages them to do, and tries to find out what brings people joy. "Some people enjoy putting stamps on envelopes, some like to speak, others enjoy fund-raising, and still others enjoy giving money," he observes.

Ron also points out the advantage of giving to a cooperative ministry like Evangelical Concern which can stretch dollars through bulk buying and through its access to food banks and warehouses that give generous discounts to a food ministry. Thus, $10 given to Evangelical Concern can feed three families for a week, and $150 will buy $1,500 worth of food. "Evangelical Concern can do ten times as much as others through its purchases. This is thrilling stuff," he says, noting that getting involved in meeting needs is basically a matter of stewardship and availability. "Do it, just do it!" he exhorts.[6]

On the national level, another effective organization is Evangelicals for Social Action (ESA). For information on resources and workshops available through ESA, write to P.O. Box 76560, Washington, D.C. 20013.

Unlimited Service Opportunities

Caring Christians who are faithfully applying the Scriptures to their lives on a daily basis will never exhaust the possibilities for caring/action ministries. As Carl F.H. Henry, a prolific author and highly respected theologian, observes:

> The biblical view declares both individual conversion and social justice to be alike indispensable. The Bible calls for personal holiness and for sweeping social changes; it refuses to substitute private religion for social responsibility or social engagement for personal commitment to God. The Bible seeks righteousness throughout

God's creation, and commands man to love God with his whole being (Matthew 22:37), to walk uprightly and to seek justice (Micah 2:7), in short, to love his neighbor as himself.[7]

Later, in the same book, *A Plea for Evangelical Demonstration*, Henry applies the biblical teaching to the individual's daily life,

The Christian prays daily, and ought to work daily, for God's will to be done on earth, as in heaven. As a citizen of two worlds he will engage actively wherever possible in the struggle for social righteousness to the full limit of personal ability and competence. Existing social structures that frustrate human freedom and public justice must be challenged. When the basic survival needs of mankind outrun the capacity or ability of voluntarism to meet them, then more adequate social legislation may helpfully serve the sore needs of mankind.[8]

Caring Christians should live out their discipleship on both the individual and the social level. While some will limit their involvement to ministries of social service, others will be called by God to challenge social structures as Christians who become personally involved in political and legislative action. As John Stott comments in *Christian Mission in the Modern World:*

If we love our neighbour as God made him, we must inevitably be concerned for his total welfare, the good of his soul, his body and his community. Moreover it is this vision of man as a social being, as well as a psycho-somatic being, which obliges us to add a *political* dimension to our social concern. Humanitarian activity cares for the casualties of a sick society. We should be concerned with preventive medicine or community health as well, which means the quest for better social structures in which peace, dignity, freedom and justice are secured for all men.[9]

Many Christians still tend to view social ministry in the community as being less important than evangelistic outreach. Consequently, a lot of time and effort has been expended explaining the relationship of these two aspects of the church's mission. I have personally found Ronald Sider's article, "Evangelism or Social Justice, Eliminating the Options," helpful because it frees Christians to recognize that both evangelism and social justice are essential aspects of the church's mission, and both are appropriate ministries for individual believers to exercise as the Lord leads. Sider concludes his article with four observations on the interrelationship of evangelism and social concern:

1. In the first place, proclamation of the biblical Gospel necessarily includes a call to repentance and turning away from all forms of sin. Sin is both personal and societal.

2. Second, the very existence of the Church as a new community where all social relationships are being redeemed has a significant impact on society, because the Church has often offered—and should always offer—a visible model of the way people can live in community in more loving and just ways.

3. Third, social action sometimes facilitates the task of evangelism . . . increasing social justice may make some people more open to the Good News . . . in that situation the act of social concern is itself truly evangelistic.

4. Fourth, a biblically-informed social action will not fail to point out that participation in social injustice is not just inhuman behavior toward one's neighbor but also sin against Almighty God.[10]

The report on Evangelism and Social Responsibility suggests a helpful distinction between social service and social action.[11] The report suggests that "social service" ministries seek to relieve human needs by ministering to individuals and families through works of mercy. "Social action," the report explains, includes attempts to remove the *causes* of human need through political and economic activity, the quest for justice, and attempts to transform the structures of society.

If caring Christians begin social service ministries within their local congregations, they may extend their ministries into the community at large, and as they become more fully involved in community-wide ministries, they may decide to become involved in the quest for social justice and to work for change in social structures as another logical extension of their commitment to biblical discipleship. "Social change is the goal for which changed individuals work for God's glory and man's good," says William Pinson.[12]

As you lead your local church out into community-wide ministries, how can your church, and the lay people of your church, do evangelism, social service, and social action?

The report on Evangelism and Social Responsibility provides some helpful guidelines. "Both personal evangelism and personal service are expressions of compassion. Both are forms of witness to Jesus Christ. And both should be sensitive responses to human need."[13] The report goes on to encourage Christians to provide food, clothing, shelter, and medical care for the needy, minister to psychological needs, and work to provide employment, teach literacy, and relieve poverty.

Commenting on social action, the report helpfully describes the wide range and variety of ministry opportunities in this area:

> The other kind of social responsibility is the quest for justice. It looks beyond persons to

structures, beyond the rehabilitation of prison inmates to the reform of the prison system, beyond improving factory conditions to securing a more participatory role for the workers, beyond caring for the poor to improving—and when necessary, transforming—the economic system (whatever it may be) and the political system (again, whatever it may be), until it facilitates their liberation from poverty and oppression.[14]

The report correctly refers to personal evangelism, social service, and social action as the *forms*, and calls individuals, small groups, parachurch groups, and local churches the *agents* of evangelism and social responsibility.

The report affirms the need for individual Christians to do both personal evangelism and personal social service. Noting that "individual Christians should be involved in both, according to their opportunities, gifts and callings."[15] And local churches must be committed to bringing the gospel to all the people in their neighborhoods, and dedicated to demonstrating a concern for their social needs as well.

Moving on to the question of involvement in political action, the report urges churches to encourage their members to become well-informed about political issues and to act according to their consciences. Adding, "Since individual action is usually limited in its effects, however, Christians should also be encouraged to form or join groups and movements which concern themselves with specific needs in society, undertake research into social issues, and organize appropriate action."[16]

If this is to happen, the churches must strive to relate biblical teaching to contemporary problems. And the report urges Christians who are community leaders, opinion formers, and decision makers—especially parents, teachers, journalists, and politicians—to explain how Christians can "fight to protect, re-establish or introduce Christian ethical values . . . . Our Christian responsibility is to get into the public debate about current issues, boldly affirm, practice and argue what the Bible teaches, and so seek to influence public opinion for Christ."[17]

Local churches must delegate the responsibility for such specialized ministries to specialized groups— evangelistic groups for evangelism, prayer groups, home Bible study groups, and study/action groups for social service and action. "As the church responds sensitively to the evangelistic needs which it perceives in its community, appropriate new groups can constantly be brought into being."[18]

Lastly, the report sketches some of the limitless possibilities for social service and social action groups in community-wide ministries.

The church needs social service groups. One may organize literacy classes with an ethnic minority, another may visit senior citizens or hospital patients or prison inmates, another may initiate a development project in a local slum area, or found a co-operative with the poor, or a club with delinquent youth, while another may offer citizens' advice or legal aid to those who cannot afford to pay for it. Again, the possibilities are almost limitless.

The church may decide to form one or more social action groups, if this is compatible with its understanding of the church's role in society. Such groups would doubtless devote a good deal of their time to study, in which they may seek the help of experts. They might take up a global problem, in order to educate themselves and (if given the opportunity) the church. Or they might address themselves to an ethical issue like abortion.

All these groups—for evangelism, social service or social action—need to relate closely to the church, reporting back regularly and seeking advice and support. In this way the ministry of the church can be greatly diversified.[19]

The community surrounding your local church is wracked with both personal and social problems. Some of them are the direct consequences of sinful behavior, others are a result of man's inhumanity to man. But whatever the causes, local churches and caring Christians cannot ignore such needs. We must reach out into the community with God's love, and go out into the community determined to make a lasting impact for Jesus' sake.

As Mother Teresa of Calcutta wisely observes:

People today are hungry for love, for understanding love which is much greater and which is the only answer to loneliness and great poverty. That is why we are able to go to countries like England and America and Australia where there is no hunger for bread. But there, people are suffering from terrible loneliness, terrible despair, terrible hatred, feeling unwanted, feeling helpless, feeling hopeless. They have forgotten how to smile, they have forgotten the beauty of the human touch. They are forgetting what is human love. They need someone who will understand and respect them.[20]

As a Christian whose life has been transformed and filled with God's love you can personally make a difference in your community. Share God's love with those in your community who hunger for love.

Listen closely to Mother Teresa, who says, "God loves you with a special love. Love others as He loves you."[21]

For Study or Discussion

1. What are the advantages of forming an organization such as Evangelical Concern in your city?

2. What is the difference between social service and social action?

3. The author asks, "As you lead your local church out into community-wide ministries, how can your church . . . do evangelism, social service and social action?" Discuss possible answers to this question as it applies to your church.

Notes

1. Lausanne Occasional Papers No. 21, Grand Rapids Report—*Evangelism and Social Responsibility an Evangelical Commitment* (Lausanne Committee for World Evangelization and the World Evangelical Fellowship, 1982), p. 50.

2. Francis Schaeffer, *The Church at the End of the 20th Century*, (Downers Grove, IL: Inter-Varsity Press, 1970), pp. 133-153.

3. Evangelical Concern of Denver, "Statement of Ministry," no date, p. 1.

4. Ibid., p. 4.

5. Evangelical Concern of Denver, *Newsletter*, April, 1983.

6. Personal interview with Dr. E. Ronald Bard, executive director, Evangelical Concern of Denver.

7. Carl F.H. Henry, *A Plea for Evangelical Demonstration* (Grand Rapids: Baker Book House, 1971), p. 107.

8. Ibid., p. 122.

9. John Stott, *Christian Mission in the Modern World* (Downers Grove, IL: Inter-Varsity Press, 1975), p. 30.

10. Ronald J. Sider, "Evangelism or Social Justice, Eliminating the Options," *Christianity Today*, October 8, 1976, pp. 26-29.

11. Lausanne Occasional Papers No. 21, pp. 43-44.

12. William M. Pinson, *Applying the Gospel*, (Nashville: Broadman Press, 1975), p. 13.

13. Lausanne Occasional Papers No. 21, p. 44.

14. Ibid., p. 45.

15. Ibid., p. 46.

16. Ibid., p. 47.

17. Ibid., p. 51.

18. Ibid., p. 54.

19. Ibid., pp. 54-55.

20. Desmond Doig, *Mother Teresa and Her Work*, (San Francisco: Harper and Row Publishers, 1976), p. 159.

21. Ibid., p. 167.

Chapter 10

Simpler Life-Styles for More Effective Outreach

"You can't enjoy the life of Jesus unless you have His life-style,"[1] says D. John Richard, executive secretary of the Evangelical Fellowship of India.

Do you want to *enjoy* the life of Jesus? If so, you must be willing to consider His life-style carefully, thoughtfully, and prayerfully.

Do you remember when a teacher of the law eagerly professed his willingness to follow Jesus anywhere? The Lord replied: "Foxes have holes and birds of the air have nests, but the Son of Man has no place to lay his head" (Matt. 8:20).

And when Jesus met the rich young ruler, who had faithfully kept the law from childhood, Jesus lovingly said, "One thing you lack . . . . Go, sell everything you have and give to the poor, and you will have treasure in heaven. Then come, follow me" (Mark 10:21). But the young man "went away sad, because he had great wealth" (Mark 10:21).

In his chapter on "New Testament Foundations for Living More Simply" in *Living More Simply*, New Testament scholar Peter Davids notes that most Christians avoid the implications of this passage by emphasizing one's attitude toward wealth rather than the idea of actually giving up wealth. "Can there be a true inward attitude without outward consequences?" asks Davids. "Is it not hypocrisy to teach one way and live another? One might suggest that the point is not wealth at all; rather we must renounce anything that comes between us and God."[2]

Davids also points out how Jesus explained to the amazed disciples that it is hard for anyone to enter the kingdom (Mark 10:24), but twice emphasizes the difficulty facing the rich person who wants to enter the kingdom—it's not impossible, but it's easier for a camel to thread a needle than for a rich man to enter the kingdom of God (Mark 10:23,25).

"We conclude," writes Davids, "that Jesus indicates two uncomfortable facts: His followers must in life as well as in attitude be detached from all that keeps them from total commitment, and wealth is one of the greatest barriers to that commitment, perhaps the greatest."[3]

Next, Davids paints an insightful portrait of Jesus' life-style—a life-style that balanced a capacity to accept both poverty and plenty from God's hand:

> Jesus, of course, was no ascetic. Even though he did fast at least once and was relatively poor himself, he glorified neither poverty nor abstention from pleasure. On the contrary, he was known as a "drunkard and a glutton," a "friend of tax-gatherers and sinner," who "ate with them." Luke in particular often presents Jesus at a meal; his disciples were criticized for *not* fasting. For him good things were to be enjoyed, but his conduct showed that he had no investment in them. They were not essential to his life-style. Thus he could wander with a band of disciples whose only guarantee of support was "the Father in heaven," living out the teaching of trust presented in Matthew 6:25-34. His life

was no search for holy poverty, but rather a joyful acceptance of both poverty and abundance
as the will of his Father.[4]

The first disciples Jesus called accepted a simple life-
style as a condition of their discipleship. But Jesus told
them they could enjoy great happiness even though
they were materially poor: "Blessed are you who are
poor, for yours is the kingdom of God" (Luke 6:20).

Many Christians turn to Matthew 5:3, and stress the
spiritual interpretation of poverty found in Matthew's
account of the Sermon on the Mount—"Blessed are the
poor in *spirit,* for theirs is the kingdom of heaven"
(Matt. 5:3, italics added). Commenting on these verses,
Dr. Rene Padilla, an associate editor of Latin America
Mission Publications and formerly the general director
of the International Fellowship of Evangelical Students
in Latin America, makes several thought-provoking
observations:

> For what does it mean to be poor in spirit if it is
> not primarily to share the outlook of the materi-
> ally poor? . . . Neither the poor nor the rich have
> a part in the Kingdom unless, regardless of
> their deprivation or material possessions, they
> are poor in spirit and as such totally dependent
> on God's grace . . . . If it is clear that Jesus did
> at times demand literal poverty as a condition of
> discipleship, why should we take it for granted
> that in our case his demand to renounce all our
> possessions should be interpreted figuratively?[5]

Jesus' own willingness to live simply, and to accept
poverty as part of His earthly life-style, sets us a challenging example. He deliberately chose a sacrificial life-
style so that He could die humbly in our place. "God
made him who had no sin to be sin for us, so that in
him we might become the righteousness of God" (2 Cor.

5:21). Because he was willing to live as a servant in real poverty, we can enjoy salvation and all of the rich spiritual blessings that are available to those who trust the Saviour personally. As Paul explains, "For you know the grace of our Lord Jesus Christ, that though he was rich, yet for your sakes he became poor, so that you through his poverty might become rich" (2 Cor. 8:9). In both attitude and life-style, we must live simple, Christlike lives of service.

If I want to enjoy the life of Jesus, I must share His life-style. And since I do want to enjoy my life with Him, I must think honestly about the questions these Scriptures bring to mind:

Will I follow Him anywhere—even if there's no place to rest?

Will I sell everything and give to the poor?

Will I joyfully accept both poverty and plenty as the will of my heavenly Father?

Will I voluntarily share the outlook of the materially poor and depend totally on God's grace?

Will I gladly give up my rightful position to serve others—practically and spiritually—so they will come to know Christ personally?

These are just a few of the questions I must face honestly as I consider Jesus' simple life-style and strive to apply both His teachings and His example in the area of life-style to my daily life. While I've raised these questions primarily for my own reflection, I trust that you will also carefully consider the Lord's example and think about how you can apply His teachings on life-style for yourself.

The recent renewal of interest in simpler life-styles among Christians worldwide was sparked, in part, by the Lausanne Covenant—a statement agreed upon by an international meeting of Christians in Lausanne, Switzerland, a decade ago. In a paragraph dealing with "The Urgency of the Evangelistic Task," the Lausanne Covenant affirms the importance of giving every person an opportunity to hear, understand, and receive the good news. Then it notes:

> All of us are shocked by the poverty of millions and disturbed by the injustices which cause it. Those of us who live in affluent circumstances accept our duty to develop a simple life-style in order to contribute more generously to both relief and evangelism.[6]

Numerous small-group meetings and several national and international Christian gatherings have taken up the discussion of the need for simpler living by Christians, as well as sharing principles, lessons, and models from individuals and communities who have developed effective ways to live more simply.

Many Christians now agree with Charles Brick's comment, "We must live more simply so that others may simply live."[7]

Others, including one Third-World Christian leader, are quick to remind Westerners that in spite of many consultations and discussions on the need for simpler life-styles among wealthy Christians, "It seems that the Third World has a franchise on the simple life-style." Our Christian brothers and sisters in the developing countries cannot afford the luxury of discussing simpler living—it is their only option. Consequently, Third-World Christians have been quicker to respond to the biblical teachings on poverty, simplicity, and community. As a result, they often understand the gospel as good news to the poor in a way that Western Christians will not so long as we live richly and luxuriously.

Simpler living in North America will not automatically improve the quality of life, prevent hunger, or eliminate need in Ethiopia, Bangladesh, or Haiti. But simpler living by many Western Christians can show the suffering members of the Body of Christ that we weep when they weep, share their pain to some degree, and are committed to life-styles that will allow us to give more to relief projects—designed to deal with emergency needs such as droughts, floods, and famines; and to give more to development projects—designed to deal with the root causes of persistent poverty caused by various social injustices, a lack of funding for long-term solutions, or not having sufficient skilled personnel or the appropriate resources to implement long-range community development proposals.

Simpler life-styles do help us identify with the poor by allowing us to experience needs similar to theirs and to learn to depend more on God. Simpler life-styles can free us from the tyranny of consumerism and materialism as a way of life. Simpler life-styles can help us rediscover the biblical emphasis on our membership and participation in a community of caring, sharing brothers and sisters. Deliberately chosen, carefully planned simpler life-styles can enable us to live on less so that we can share our surplus with others and give more to evangelism, relief, and development projects worldwide.

John Stott has written that Christians should seek equal opportunity for all people through education, medical care, housing, nutrition, and trade so that every person can fully develop his or her God-given potential. And he is right.

Stott then makes some practical suggestions that deserve our careful consideration:

> God may be calling more Christian people than hear and respond to his call to give their lives in the service of the poor and powerless, in practical philanthropy or Third World development, in politics, or in economics . . . . We have to feel what Jesus felt—the pangs of the hungry, the alienation of the powerless, and the indignities of the wretched of the earth. For ultimately, the unacceptable inequalities between North and

South are neither political nor economic, but rather moral. Until we feel more indignation about worldwide social injustice and strong compassion for worldwide human suffering, I seriously doubt we shall be moved to take action.[8]

In the same helpful *Christianity Today* article, Stott suggests several specific steps we can take to demonstrate the reality of our commitment to a simper lifestyle:

Nearly all of us drink tea and coffee, probably sweeten it with sugar, eat bananas and wear textile clothing. We cannot enjoy these things responsibly if we remain indifferent to the wages and living conditions of those who produce them, and to the trade agreements by which they have become available to us. So we should take steps to find out. Does the daily paper we read have adequate Third World coverage? Do we subscribe to a magazine devoted to Third World needs? . . . More personally still, could we make friends with a Third World citizen or travel to some region of the Third World in order to educate ourselves at first hand? Or could we offer ourselves for short-term service in a developing country? And does our church have a "world development group" in addition to a "world mission group," whose responsibility is to inform itself and to keep the congregation informed? . . . Most communities have pressure groups, which are seeking to influence public opinion and increase public concern about development issues. They could benefit from a Christian contribution to their thought and action.[9]

While John Stott has led many of the discussions on the need to return to a simpler, more biblical life-style, he is not alone. In 1980, for example, eighty-five Christian leaders from twenty-five countries agreed upon "An Evangelical Commitment to Simple Life-style" at a meeting in London, England. All local churches and all lay persons who want to meet practical needs in Christ's name should study this well-thought-out statement carefully.

Section 5 on Personal Life-style includes these convicting words:

> Our Christian obedience demands a simple life-style, irrespective of the needs of others. Nevertheless, the facts that 800 million people are destitute and that about 10,000 die of starvation every day make any other life-style indefensible.
>
> While some of us have been called to live among the poor, and others to open our homes to the needy, all of us are determined to develop a simpler life-style. We intend to reexamine our income and expenditure, in order to manage on less and give away more. We lay down no rules or regulations, for either ourselves or others. Yet we resolve to renounce waste and oppose extravagance in personal living, clothing and housing, travel and church buildings.[10]

The same section also considers the need for churches in the West to learn from Third-World churches:

> Those of us who belong to the West need the help of our Third World brothers and sisters in evaluating our standards of spending. Those of us who live in the Third World acknowledge that

we too are exposed to the temptation to covet-
ousness. So we need each other's understanding, encouragement and prayers.[11]

Jun Vencer, a Christian leader in the Philippines,
challenged the leaders of several North American relief
and development agencies to reexamine their relationships with local churches during two thought-provoking addresses at a meeting of the Association of Evangelical Relief and Development Organizations in 1982.
"It is only through the church that any other ministry
will find meaning within the plan of God and the will of
God. What we do must be done within His will," said
Vencer.[12] In a day when parachurch organizations and
agencies have taken the lead in relief and development
work worldwide, local churches and parachurch agencies must consider Vencer's statement carefully. Can
local churches recover the initiative for planning, organizing, and implementing relief and development ministries worldwide? And will Western congregations and
communities be willing to work cooperatively under the
leadership of national Christians and organizations?

Lay people who want to explore alternative Christian
life-styles in order to work more effectively for relief and
development as well as evangelism must look for opportunities to do so within their local churches. And the
local churches must provide forums, ministry opportunities, and support for mission-minded lay men and
women. When this happens, the local church will be
able to minister more effectively at home and abroad.
Instead of allowing parachurch organizations to dominate relief and development ministries worldwide—as
they do now—the local churches could return to a more
central role in the effort to meet needs. Western
churches must creatively form sister-church relationships with local churches in the developing countries.
Living more simply today will help church members in
the West prepare themselves for a servant-role in coop-

erative ministries with churches in the Third World tomorrow.

As with many of the biblical themes we've encountered, when you practice simpler living in your situation, it will create opportunities for you to serve and minister more effectively—in your neighborhood, city, nation, and even cross-culturally if the Lord leads you to serve Him in that way.

Some may question an emphasis on simpler living, but simpler living is an essential aspect of biblical obedience and witness. As Jim Wallis, editor of *Sojourners* magazine, observes,

> The question of the Christian style of life in the world is the crucial point where the truth and the power of the gospel will be most severely tested. Theology and doctrine have no power apart from a style of life in the world that is consistent with what is believed . . . . A Christian is more than someone who wants to change things; a Christian is someone who is being changed . . . . The key to the kingdom is faithfulness in following Christ daily. Therefore, the Christian style of life is not an objective but a consequence of obedience and witness. The Christian life-style is a life of testimony.[13]

Speaking at Young Life's Summer Institute of Theology in 1982, Wallis pointed out that today, especially in North America, Christians live as materialists who have little experience with the Holy Spirit, and as individualists who have little experience of community.

"What do we Christians have to explain to the world about the way we live?" asks Wallis. He adds that in New Testament times the believers expected to be questioned about the reason for their distinctive life-style (see 1 Pet. 3:15). Today, says Wallis, the question is no longer being asked. Yet a distinctive Christian life-style would be immediately recognized by believers and nonbelievers alike, he concludes.[14]

Christians in North America can return to a distinctive, simpler, Christian life-style if we will commit ourselves to a caring, sharing, open life-style in communities of faith in which we will share all of our life with our brothers and sisters and with the strangers, outcasts, and lost people of our world.

Simpler living can thus promote evangelistic outreach as well as practical ministries focusing on relief and development issues. Each believer, each family, each local church must learn to think biblically about every area of their personal and corporate life-style so this will happen. And as individuals and as local communities of believers we must base our actions upon how the Lord directs us individually and corporately.

Ron Sider made some excellent suggestions on how to practice simpler living at the International Consultation on Simple Life-style. Read over this selection of his suggestions, and act on those which you can apply to your personal situation or within your local church's life and ministry:

1. The Holy Spirit will guide individual Christians as they prayerfully seek His will by studying both the Bible and the newspaper in the context of Christian community.

2. A congregation could decide, at its annual business meeting, that in the course of the next two years it would try to help each member of the congregation discover what life-style God wills for them.

3. Each person or family should prayerfully decide what to do for themselves. But surely the wisdom and loving insight of other sisters and brothers should provide helpful assistance to uncover blind spots, selfishness, and neglected alternatives.

4. Live among the poor—the rural or urban poor in either the developed nations or the Third World.

5. Literally hundreds of thousands of Christians

ought to move (in groups) to the poor sections of large cities.

6. Many ought to live in suburban areas. But it will be possible to sustain a simple life-style there only if communities of Christians committed to a simple life-style for the sake of evangelism and justice can be created.

7. Perhaps denominational or interdenominational agencies could develop structures to enable individual congregations to become a sister congregation to a local church in a developing country.[15]

Specific, personal life-style decisions are based on biblical convictions, personal values, family traditions and practices, and peer group influences. Decision-making processes on personal life-style issues should include a careful consideration of such things as our purpose, motive, inner attitudes, alternative ways to meet needs or accomplish goals, global perspective, and relevant biblical teachings, writes Sider.

Even simply asking questions like, Do I *need* it? Do I *really* need it? and, Do I really need it *now*? will prevent many wasteful decisions and help us to be better stewards of our finances.

Here are a few more helpful guidelines my friend, Paul Mason—who served with his wife, Karen, as a teacher in a mission school in Pakistan—developed for one of our church's missions conferences:

1. All we have belongs to God. We are His stewards for 100 percent not just 10 percent.

2. Value people more than things. Use things for people, not vice versa.

3. Develop a pilgrim mentality. Earth is not our home—we are on the frontlines of a battle. Live like it, spend like it.

4. Choose to be patient. We have eternity and do not need to grab all the "gusto" now.

5. Give cheerfully. Our money will often go further in the Third World.

6. Provide for your family. Providing does not mean spoiling, and it includes waiting, sharing, and other spiritual values lacking in a materialistic society.

7. Remind yourself of the poor. Live near enough to see them.

8. Voluntary simplicity is psychologically much different from forced poverty. Think of it as a higher life-style than materialism.

9. Be a peer leader for simplicity. Let brother "Jones" follow you.

10. Repair, recycle, restore, reuse, renew and care for what you have. Waste not, want not.[16]

Developing a simpler life-style gives us a way to follow Christ more authentically, demonstrate solidarity with the poor, and begin an educational process so that our discipleship will not remain limited to personal piety. As Christians, we can learn about, experience, and demonstrate God's compassionate concern for every area of life and every person. While simpler living has many personal benefits, it can also lead, as a result of experience and education, to a commitment to work for justice and development through churches, parachurch agencies and personal efforts. Those who hear God's call to work for development as Christians will find the following statement of intent, from a conference on the theology of development, a helpful resource for discussion, reflection, and action:

We recognize that the Bible teaches that the mission of the church includes the proclamation of the gospel and the demonstration of its relevance by working for community development and social change.

We recognize that the church is called to work for that justice in society which God wills and to help people to enjoy the fullness of life which is God's purpose for all people.

We recognize that in order to engage in social

change and model the relationships it commends for society, the church must exhibit total dependence on the transforming power of the Holy Spirit of God.

In the light of this understanding of Scripture we resolve with God's help to live out the full Christian gospel and to apply it to the needy situations in which we find ourselves.

We resolve in the company of others within the church, to study more deeply the current social, political and economic issues, which are so heavily influencing the lives of the world's population.

We resolve to change many of the attitudes that we find within ourselves which contribute to poverty and injustice.

We resolve to place greater trust in God and greater trust in each other in order to build relationships which will encourage and strengthen us in our common task to relieve poverty and injustice.

We resolve to encourage, by all the peaceful and constructive means available to us, the poor and oppressed who are seeking to establish a position of dignity and self-worth.

Finally we resolve to reconsider the use of the resources which God has given us, in order that such resources may contribute more effectively to God's kingdom and righteousness, love and justice.[17]

Simpler life-styles are essential for all who would accomplish such worthwhile objectives. And simpler life-styles are rooted in the Scriptures. As the followers of Jesus of Nazareth today, we must consider His example of living simply and ask ourselves again: How should we then live?

Consider Canadian John White's description of the

benefits that will result from a decision to live more simply:

> The Lord Christ places demands upon his followers which it is their privilege to respond to. His demands differ from those of earthly captains. He insists they let him transform the hours they spend on common tasks—washing, dressing, studying, buying, selling or on working for earthly masters—so that these activities henceforth be performed as acts of worship ardently rendered to his glory. Then he opens new and golden hours that were once vainly wasted so that now they may be devoted to feeding the hungry, clothing the naked, healing the sick, opening the eyes of the blind, comforting the sorrowing and proclaiming his blood-bought liberty for slaves of sin.[18]

For Study or Discussion

1. Read Matthew 10:37-39. What does Jesus mean when He says that "whosoever loses his life for my sake will find it"? How does this same idea apply to Jesus' words in Matthew 19:21? How practical is it for all of us to sell everything we have and give it to the poor? Are the poor and poverty-stricken closer to God than the rich? Read Matthew 6:25-34, especially verse 33. What should we seek first? How does this thought fit in with the author's admonition to "seek a simpler life-style"?

2. List some things you can do without this week that would make for a "simpler life-style." What would be an approximate dollar figure that you would save? Where can you apply that amount of dollars to alleviate world suffering? Will you do it? Even if it doesn't represent much money it is more than you gave last week. What will you do next week?

3. Read and discuss the quotation from the Lausanne Covenant on page 179.

4. Explain the terms "relief" and "development." Is your church presently involved in both of these ministries, or is there a way to significantly increase your involvement in one of these areas?

5. If you were asked to launch a "world development group" in your church, how would you begin?

6. How can your congregation become more informed about the needs of Christians and churches in the developing nations?

Notes

1. D. John Richard, as quoted in "Social Justice Barrier," *Christianity Today*, November 16, 1979, p. 60.

2. Peter H. Davids, *Living More Simply* (Downers Grove, IL: Inter-Varsity Press, 1980), p. 43.

3. Ibid., p. 43.

4. Ibid., pp. 43-44.

5. Rene Padilla, in *Life-style in the Eighties* edited by Ronald J. Sider (Philadelphia: The Westminster Press, 1982), pp. 57-62.

6. J.D. Douglas, ed., *Let the Earth Hear His Voice* (Minneapolis: World Wide Publications, 1975), p. 6.

7. Charles Brick, as quoted in "The World as Monastery," *Sojourners*, October, 1979, p. 29.

8. John Stott, "The Just Demands of Economic Inequality," *Christianity Today*, May 23, 1980, p. 30.

9. Ibid., p. 30.

10. *An Evangelical Commitment to Simple Life-style*, (World Evangelical Fellowship, 1980) sect. 5, "Personal Life-style."

11. Ibid., sect. 5.

12. Jun Vencer, personal notes taken during his address to the Association of Evangelical Relief and Development Organizations in Colorado Springs in November, 1982.

13. Jim Wallis, *Agenda for a Biblical People* (San Francisco: Harper and Row Publishers, 1976), pp. 35,38.

14. Jim Wallis, personal notes taken during a message given during the Young Life Summer Institute of Theology in July, 1982.

15. Ronald J. Sider, ed., *Life-style in the Eighties* (Philadelphia: The Westminster Press, 1982), pp. 33-35.

16. Paul Mason, "World Evangelism and Simple Life-styles," unpublished paper, pp. 1-4.

17. Ronald J. Sider, ed., *Evangelicals and Development: Towards a Theology of Social Change*, Contemporary Issues on Social Ethics, vol. 2, (Exeter: The Paternoster Press, and World Evangelical Fellowship, 1981), pp. 15-16.

18. John White, *The Golden Cow*, (Downers Grove, IL: Inter-Varsity Press, 1979), pp. 49-50.

Chapter 11

Build World Vision in Your Local Church

If you are teaching an adult Sunday School class, or leading a home Bible study, try a simple quiz on your class or study group members. Select the names of half a dozen missionaries who are supported by your church and serving in six different foreign countries. Then ask your students to locate the countries where those missionaries serve on a world map. As you'll probably discover from the results of such a quiz, world knowledge—even basic geography—is often woefully weak among Christians.

When I first arrived in the United States, many people had no idea where my homeland—New Zealand—was located. One person thought it was close to Iceland, many thought it was part of Australia, but very few North Americans knew exactly where New Zealand is. And it's quite likely that very few members of your church will know precisely where in the world the missionaries you support are located.

How can you, a lay person in a local church, help your fellow Christians become more world-conscious? Once again, you must model a concern for the whole world if you want to help others develop a similar concern. Begin with yourself, and prayerfully ask God to help you develop an accurate, biblical, and contemporary *world vision*.

As you've already seen from our study of the church of the first century, that church had a world vision. The early church's vision resulted in action. The early Christians became known as the people who turned their world upside down. Starting in Jerusalem, reaching out into Judea and Samaria, they eventually affected all of the then known world. And Christians today can have a similar impact. *Every* believer can apply the Acts 1:8 principle personally, and demonstrate a personal world vision which begins by influencing people locally, but eventually reaches out to influence the whole world for Jesus Christ. You can develop a stimulating world vision of your own that will give your life direction, purpose, and lasting significance.

Just as individuals can develop a personal vision for the world, so can families. And local churches must strive to develop a global understanding of God's work in the world today and tomorrow. In this chapter, therefore, I'd like to make some suggestions for individuals, families and local churches who want to develop a vision for the whole world. Each suggestion can be flexibly applied according to individual, family, and church needs and opportunities. You should add to these suggestions your own ideas for getting to know the world better. Learn from your own experience, and learn from others who display a world vision. This is such a challenging concept that it's impossible to exhaust the possibilities. Every Christian can keep learning about the world and keep growing his or her world vision for a lifetime.

If you've already developed your heart for the world, use these suggestions to encourage other Christians to get the whole world on their hearts. Teach others how to think globally while acting locally. But if you do not know how to view the world from God's perspective, use this chapter to help you begin a lifelong personal study of what the Scriptures teach about God's love for the whole world. Get a *world* vision!

How You Can Develop a World Vision

Learn from others. One person, a former missionary, taught me more about world vision than anyone else. Whenever he spoke at conferences, and whenever I talked with him personally, he shared something fresh and stimulating about what God was doing *worldwide.* Although he had many natural opportunities to learn about the world during his missionary travels, this man also gave himself to the study of worldwide needs, trends, and opportunities. He read widely and personally modeled a constant hunger to learn more about the past, present, and future of the Christian movement worldwide. My own world vision developed, in part, because of the way in which the breadth and depth of his world vision sparked my imagination. By his life this missionary modeled for me what it means to have a world vision. And you can learn how to cultivate your world vision from others too.

Missionaries who visit your church, a pastor, a Sunday School teacher, someone who has lived and worked overseas, anyone who's excited about reaching all of the peoples of the world with the good news can share their world vision with you. Ask questions, listen attentively, and learn all you can every time God brings a world-minded individual into your life. Pray that God will often give you opportunities to meet such people and learn from them.

Learn on your own. Once you whet your appetite and begin to enjoy the heart-stretching, mind-stimulating joys of learning about peoples and customs in other cultures, you'll want to keep learning on your own. How can you do that?

First, read your Bible carefully—make a note of passages you read that describe God's own concern for the whole world. John 3:16 is the best-known verse about

God's love for the whole world.

Second, watch the world news carefully on television, and read the world news regularly in daily newspapers and weekly newsmagazines. Collect helpful resources as you read. Pray as you watch and read the world news. Look up the locations of the countries you're learning about. Use an atlas to pinpoint the locations of foreign cities on a map of the particular country you are researching.

Third, read Christian magazines that interpret world events and news from a biblical perspective. Look for Christian books that will help you to understand life in other cultures. Read and pray over newsletters from individual missionaries, churches, and other organizations working overseas.

Fourth, share what you learn. Just as you receive knowledge from others, so you can share what you learn with others. When you've learned about a specific need in a particular country, explain what you've learned to someone else. In your small-group Bible study, or in your caring ministry group, talk about current events and pray together for Christians in the nations and cities you are learning about in your personal world studies. And pray for the unreached peoples in those countries—those who've not yet had an opportunity to hear the gospel in a way that they can understand.

Pray for world needs on your own and with others. Ask God to give you a world vision. Ask Him to give you a deep and lasting personal desire to be practically involved in taking the whole gospel to the whole person in the whole world. Commit yourself to praying daily for another country. Perhaps you can begin by praying for one missionary you know and for his or her ministry in *one* foreign country. Or you can pray daily for the unreached peoples by using a tool like the *Daily Prayer Guide*[1] published by the U.S. Center for World Mission in Pasadena, California. Or you can use Patrick Johnstone's *Operation World*.² Whatever approach you use, be sure to pray that you will always be eager to learn about all that God is doing through His people in the world today.

As you learn and pray about world needs today, you will also be able to anticipate world needs tomorrow. This will help you stay in touch with changing conditions worldwide which may affect the progress of the gospel in some countries. You can pray that God will raise up committed people to plant the good news in those countries which are currently open to the gospel. You'll pray more intelligently, too, because your world study will help you know that some countries do not welcome full-time missionaries any longer. You will focus your prayers for those countries on the national Christian leaders and national churches, asking God to multiply them and encourage them in their strategic service for Him. And you will also pray that God will allow lay people—Christian professionals, business people, teachers, doctors, nurses, engineers, technicians, mechanics, and lay workers of all kinds to find jobs in many of the countries which are closed to traditional mission efforts.

You can pray like this on your own, but pray with others in a small group as well. Your group prayer times will stimulate each group member's world vision. Together you will be able to develop a broader vision for the world. And praying about world needs with a small group of friends will reinforce your personal commitment to do what you can to help reach the world for Christ.

Every individual Christian can learn world vision from others, learn on his or her own, and pray alone or with others about world needs and opportunities. If praying for the world is not yet something you do regularly, take five minutes right now to ask God to give you a world vision. Pray that He will help you to think globally and act locally as a concerned and committed Christian.

How Families Can Develop a World Vision

Cheryl and I have already started to help our three sons to develop a world vision—even during their pre-school years. As a family, we enjoy inviting guests from other countries to stay in our home. Our children have enjoyed sitting in on missionaries' reports, slides, and films about their ministries in other lands. We've encouraged our boys to watch the world news with us on television, and we use a set of encyclopedias regularly to help them learn more about the geography, cultures, and peoples of the world. As much as possible, we share how we are involved in missions with them. We know that one day the Lord may call us or them to serve Him in another culture, so we've tried to do things now that will help us to be ready when that day comes.

Hospitality is one of the best ways a family can get a feel for the rich variety of races, languages, cultures, and customs of today's world. And now, especially in some parts of the United States, it's becoming much easier to meet people from a different cultural background from your own. Today, your family can meet blacks, Hispanics, Vietnamese, Japanese, Koreans, or people from almost any nationality, right in your own hometown, suburb, or city. The United States is populated with such a great diversity of peoples that you can learn about the world's countries and peoples without ever leaving home.

Of course, this opportunity to learn about foreign cultures without traveling overseas should also be viewed by individuals, families, and churches as a great missionary-training opportunity. If you, or some other member of your family, want to learn what it's like to be a missionary to people from another country who speak a foreign language, you can start learning right where you are. And families have many natural opportunities to invite other families over and to start getting to know each other informally over coffee, a potluck supper, a backyard barbecue, a child's birthday party, or just a brief neighborly visit with the new family on your block. Yes, you and your family can have a world-changing ministry if you are willing to start where you are and do what you can.

Many families get their first taste of such a cross-cultural ministry by hosting international students in their home for a few days or weeks at a time. The joys of learning about foreign countries while hosting students from overseas are endless. Try it as a family. You'll like it!

If the Lord leads your family to continue your involvement, and you want to become regularly involved with internationals, International Students Incorporated can give you more training, direction, and suggestions for sharing your home, your family's love, and your faith with international students. Remember, these men and women often return to their own countries and eventually become key leaders in government, education, and industry. Your home can become a highly strategic ministry base for reaching out to the future leaders of many foreign countries.

My own parents always set an example for me in this area. While I was in high school, my family hosted a Japanese high school student who wanted to attend school in New Zealand for a year. And my father demonstrated the value of learning foreign languages, because he taught himself how to speak at least two foreign languages fluently. He learned Dutch from a Dutch naval officer during four years as a prisoner of war in the second world war. Later in life he taught himself German, and became fluent enough and knowledgeable enough that he was able to teach others German also. Towards the end of his life, my dad was learning to read and write Japanese by correspondence from a nearby university. In these practical ways my father modeled for me how anyone can learn another language if they are willing to work at it. Because of the close friendship between my dad and the Dutch naval officer, I grew up in a home where Dutch was often spoken. As well as visiting Holland as a child, I have very fond memories of visits in New Zealand with Dutch families in whose homes I developed a taste for delicious Dutch refreshments—from soup to homemade pastries served with tasty coffee. All of these experiences gave me a deep personal appreciation for learning about the people, culture, and customs of foreign countries. And this distinctive feature of my family's home life is something I cherish and want to pass on to my own children.

As you think about your family, first evaluate what you are already doing to encourage a world vision among family members. Then plan one or two new activities that will help your family develop a global perspective. Discuss the day's world news together, for example, and pray for the churches, national Christians, and missionaries in the countries featured. The news may suggest some very specific, very real needs or concerns to pray about too. Be sure you locate the countries you pray for on a world map or in an atlas. If you have an encyclopedia or some other reference book, read about the people and culture of the country you pray for as well. Perhaps your family can host a visiting missionary or an international student who's coming to your town soon. Or you can visit an ethnic neighborhood in your own city to sample some distinctive food, listen to a different language, and learn about how people from other countries are adapting to life in your local community. Activities like these are all simple stepping-stones towards building a lasting concern for the whole world in your family. But they can make a difference, and in these ways you can become a person who is in touch with what God is doing throughout the world. Start enlarging your family's world vision today!

How a Church Can Expand Its World Vision

Local churches have a special responsibility to teach members how to have a world vision. On every recorded occasion that Jesus commissioned the disciples after His resurrection, He emphasized the goal of world outreach. The early disciples turned their neighborhood, cities, countries, and world upside down. The early church's world vision motivated a worldwide outreach. The early church helped fulfill Christ's Great Commission because they had a world vision. Your local church must develop the same alertness to global opportunities and needs. And you can personally model world vision and encourage other members of your local church to develop a vital world vision of their own. If you do, and your family members regularly share their excitement about being world Christians with other members of your congregation, you can affect your local church's missionary impact.

One of the best ways to encourage other church members to develop a world vision is to teach a Sunday School class on world missions which includes some history of missions and discussions of contemporary opportunities and needs. You should also provide opportunities for your church-supported missionaries to share regular, in-depth reports of their ministries with your congregation. Use all of your mission-minded people to broaden the whole church's awareness of missions today. Do not leave the support of your local church's missionary program to a few faithful missions' committee members. Mobilize your entire congregation for missions.

An awareness of contemporary missions and changing conditions and opportunities in various countries must become a natural part of the total life and witness of a local church. The Acts 1:8 model instructs local churches to begin reaching the world by ministering in their Jerusalem. Your church can begin reaching the world in its immediate neighborhood. Effective lifestyles of evangelism and compassionate social service in your local area are the essential foundations for a global ministry. Apply what you learn where you are, and move out in ever-widening circles of ever-expand-ing influence. Your local church can become as effective in doing missions locally and globally as the local church in Jerusalem was during the first century.

As Frank Tillapaugh wisely notes in *The Church Unleashed,* "People must grasp the fact that the church *is* missions; the church just doesn't support missions."[3]

What are some practical ways a local church can deepen or create a world vision among its members? Here are a few suggestions your church can use and add to:

1. Your pastor can preach a series of messages on world needs and opportunities and how your church can become involved.
2. Have a regular Sunday School class on the his-tory of missions with an added emphasis on cur-rent opportunities and developments in missions worldwide.
3. Have a special world missions emphasis often (at least once a year) but consider drawing attention to missions every month or even every week in some way.
4. Share accurate, up-to-date literature, news, and reports from the missionaries your church sup-ports.
5. Bring world missions specialists in to speak in your local church whenever possible.
6. Invite national Christian leaders from other countries to minister to your members, especially during any week-long missions and Bible confer-ences.
7. Encourage the formation of world study/discus-sion groups.
8. Constantly emphasize the need to follow the Acts 1:8 model in all of your local church ministries.
9. Encourage your members to get involved with

international students in local schools and colleges.

10. Borrow experts from parachurch organizations to train your members for worldwide ministry.
11. Start learning about the world in ethnic neighborhoods in your city.
12. Teach people how to study the world as well as the Word.
13. Do it! Cultivate a world vision among your members and reach out locally, nationally, and internationally in all of the ways God enables you to.

These suggestions have been purposefully selected because they are simple, attainable application steps that any local church can take. Once you begin the exciting process of building a world vision among your local church members, God will multiply your efforts. Your local church will become a body of people who think, act, and minister both locally and globally for God's glory.

The Biblical Basis for a World Vision

Whether you want to acquire a personal world vision, deepen your family's commitment to reaching the world, or encourage your local church to become more world-oriented in its life and ministry, you'll find the Scriptures are filled with passages describing God's love for His world and His desire to reach all peoples everywhere with the good news of the gospel. Study the Scriptures for yourself by noting references to "the world," "earth," "nations," and "people/s." I've included a few of the best known Scriptures on world vision in this chapter, but I want to encourage you to do your own Bible study as well.

A world study, combining your personal Bible study with current events, news, and feature reports, church and missionary newsletters and other background reading, can be an exciting personal project. And you can share the results of your studies with friends, family, and your local church. So start a Bible study on the world today, and keep a file handy for selected news clippings, your own notes, and other references also.

World Vision in the Old Testament

"In the beginning God created the heavens and the earth" (Gen. 1:1). As the Creator of the universe, God has a special love for the world and all of its peoples. The Scriptures reveal the start of God's special relationship with the whole world, and the Scriptures anticipate the "healing of the nations" (Rev. 22:2) and describe the new heavens, new earth, and the new city that God will create in the future. There, "the throne of God and of the Lamb will be in the city, and his servants will serve him" (Rev. 22:3). In between the first and last pages of the Bible, you can observe how God reaches out to His people through His prophets, His Scriptures, and His Son. Always, He has the whole world in mind. And if we are to faithfully represent Him today, we must have a world vision.

God repeatedly reminded the nation of Israel that while they had been called to a special covenant relationship with Him, the whole earth belonged to Him and was designed to be a showcase for God's glory (Exod. 19:5-6, Num. 14:20-21). When God called Abram (later renamed Abraham), He told him that He wanted to bless "all peoples on earth" (Gen. 12:3) through him and through his descendants.

Although the chosen nation became preoccupied with its own affairs, a few individual leaders like David and King Solomon had a broader vision. Solomon, for example, prayed for foreigners who would hear about God through His people's witness and pray to Him. "Do whatever the foreigner asks of you," Solomon prayed, "so that *all the peoples of the earth may know your name and fear you*" (1 Kings 8:43, italics added).

In many of his psalms, David, too, proclaimed the Lord's kingship over *all* the nations. "Ask of me, and I will make the nations your inheritance, the ends of the earth your possession" (Ps. 2:8) he wrote in a messianic psalm. And David repeats his theme in Psalm 22:27-28, "All the ends of the earth will remember and turn to the Lord, and all the families of the nations will bow down before him, for dominion belongs to the Lord and he rules over the nations." While David's writings also emphasize God's special relationship with the people of the covenant, David knew that his God was King "over all the earth" (Ps. 47:2). And in Psalm 67:1-2 he combines a prayer for national blessing with a prayer that God will make Himself known everywhere. "May God be gracious to us and bless us and make his face shine upon us; may your ways be known on earth, your salvation among all nations."

Through the prophets' ministries, God repeated His concern for all of the world's peoples: "Turn to me and be saved, all you ends of the earth; for I am God, and there is no other" (Isa. 45:22). And individual prophets glimpsed a time when "the earth will be filled with the knowledge of the glory of the Lord, as the waters cover the sea" (Hab. 2:14).

The Old Testament expressions of God's world concern reach their climax in the "servant Songs" penned by Isaiah (Isa. 42:1-4; 49:1-6; 50:4-9; 52:13—53:12). Isaiah 49:1-6 has been appropriately described as the heart of the Old Testament, and it also captures God's heart for the whole world.

> Listen to me, you islands;
>   hear this you distant nations:
> Before I was born the Lord called me;
>   from my birth he has made mention of my name.
> He made my mouth like a sharpened sword,
>   in the shadow of his hand he hid me;
> he made me into a polished arrow
>   and concealed me in his quiver.

He said to me, "You are my servant,
   Israel, in whom I will display my splendor."
But I said, "I have labored to no purpose;
   I have spent my strength in vain and for nothing.
Yet what is due me is in the Lord's hand,
   and my reward is with my God."
And now the Lord says—
   he who formed me in the womb to be his servant
to bring Jacob back to him
   and gather Israel to himself,
for I am honored in the eyes of the Lord
   and my God has been my strength—
he says:
   "It is too small a thing for you to be my servant
   to restore the tribes of Jacob
   and bring back those of Israel I have kept.
I will also make you a light for the Gentiles,
   that you may bring my salvation to the ends
   of the earth" (Isa. 49:1-6).

World Vision in the New Testament

In the New Testament the servant theme characterized Jesus' ministry (Mark 10:45), and motivated the early apostles to reach out beyond their home base in Jerusalem to fulfill their commission to "go and make disciples of all nations" (Matt. 28:19). When Paul and Barnabas announced they would concentrate on reaching the Gentiles with the gospel (Acts 13:46), Paul quoted Isaiah 49:6 to explain their decision: "This is what the Lord has commanded us: 'I have made you a light for the Gentiles, that you may bring salvation to the ends of the earth' " (Acts 13:47). Paul applied Isaiah's words to himself, and he had a world-changing ministry. This same world vision can motivate you to have a worldwide ministry today as an individual, with your family, and through your local church.

By carefully studying Jesus' life you will observe a pattern you can follow in your ministry. Begin at home, right where you are, then move out into your neighborhood. As your spheres of influence multiply and enlarge, you can have a personal ministry in your country and, through those you influence, in many foreign countries as well. Yes, you can help to reach the world for Christ.

Consider these New Testament examples of a local church, a couple, and an individual who all made a lasting ministry impact in their time because they were committed to helping to reach the whole world.

Although the church in Thessalonica experienced severe suffering, the fellowship became "a model to all the believers in Macedonia and Achaia. The Lord's message rang out from you not only in Macedonia and Achaia—your faith in God has become known everywhere" (1 Thess. 1:7-8). This local church was commended by Paul because of its outreach, and churches today can follow its example.

Aquila and Priscilla were tentmakers by trade, and they shared their home and their trade with Paul (Acts 18:3). Later, they traveled with him to Syria (Acts 18:18). As well as supporting the apostle in his ministry, this couple also ministered to Apollos—an educated man with a deep knowledge of the Scriptures (Acts 18:24-26). Families today can learn from the example of Aquila and Priscilla by sharing their homes and resources with traveling missionaries who need rest, refreshment, or financial support. Those who do this will grow spiritually through the relationships they form, just as Aquila and Priscilla grew through their personal relationship with Paul. Like Aquila and Priscilla, families today will be able to share what they learn with others.

Paul has always been a motivating example of one individual whose whole life was dedicated to spreading the good news. And his example can motivate you today. Although Paul was perhaps the greatest pioneer missionary in the first century, he never rested on his past accomplishments. Instead, he focused his efforts on reaching the unreached. As he told the Christians in Rome, he planned and prayed for the opportunity to journey beyond Rome to Spain—an ambition that may not have been fulfilled in his lifetime. Nevertheless, Paul's personal commitment to spreading the gospel rings clearly through his letter to the Romans and can inspire you to help spread the gospel worldwide. Consider Paul's example, and resolve to dedicate your life to the same great vision—a world vision—of helping to spread the whole gospel for the whole person in the whole world. "So from Jerusalem all the way around to Illyricum, I have fully proclaimed the gospel of Christ. It has always been my ambition to preach the gospel where Christ was not known, so that I would not be building on someone else's foundation" (Rom. 15:19-20).

For Study or Discussion

1. In this chapter the author lists several ways you can develop world vision. What are these? As you list them, check the ones you are now practicing. Set some definite plans to begin putting the others into practice.

2. How can you help your family develop world vision as a family?

3. What does your church do to make its members aware of their world opportunities? Suggest other practical ways that will increase world awareness among your church members.

4. How would you describe God's "world vision"? How do you think He sees the world today?

5. Which verse or Scripture passage motivates you to cultivate you own world vision? Share your favorite passage with a friend or your discussion group or class

and explain your reasons for selecting that passage.

6. Reread Romans 15:19-20 and write a one sentence personal application based on Paul's statement.

Notes

1. *Daily Prayer Guide,* available from the U.S. Center for World Mission, 1605 E. Elizabeth Street, Pasadena, California, 91104.

2. Patrick Johnstone, *Operation World,* STL Books, Waynesboro, GA 30380.

3. Frank Tillapaugh, *The Church Unleashed,* (Ventura, CA: Regal Books, 1982), p. 220.

Chapter 12

Start Where You Are

You are a Christian lay person, and God is giving you a burden to develop a caring ministry to meet physical and material needs around you. Where should you begin? The place to begin is right where you are. Ask God for an opportunity to launch a caring ministry within your local church if such a ministry doesn't already exist.

Your local church is the best place to launch a caring ministry because the local church is the vehicle through which God wants to display His great love in our needy world. Through the church, He wants "to bring all things in heaven and on earth together under one head, even Christ" (Eph. 1:10). The local church, under the lordship of Jesus Christ, creatively shares the good news of salvation with lost men and women and invites them to join the community of the King. The church is God's family on earth, and all of our relationships ought to reflect the marvelous breadth, length, depth, and height of the love of Christ (see Eph. 3:18-19).

Jesus stressed the importance of love within the Christian community while He was still with His disciples. He said the believers' love for one another would be one of their most powerful evangelistic strategies. After demonstrating His humble style of loving service by washing the disciples' feet, Jesus said: "A new commandment I give you: Love one another. As I have loved you, so you must love one another. All men will know that you are my disciples if you love one another" (John 13:34-35).

Today, we need to recover a Christlike love that cares, shares, and serves those in need within our own fellowship. Our love must not be confined to ourselves, however; we must cultivate the kind of love which also reaches out to hurting men and women in the non-Christian world in Christ's name. When non-believers observe an authentic, Christlike love in action, they will want to learn more about the Christian life. But if we do not demonstrate an attractive, loving style of life, they may never see Christ—and they may never care to listen to His people's message.

A simple, joyful life of love will enable you to begin a caring ministry. Love God with all your heart, and your neighbor as yourself. If you begin to apply this principle today, right where you are, you will become the kind of caring Christian God uses to motivate others to serve needy individuals out of love for Him.

Begin in Your Local Church

Sometimes we assume that the place to begin caring for others is in the local community, beyond the local church. But this can be a mistake. Your local church is the place to begin a caring ministry for two quite practical reasons.

First, it is far too easy to overlook needy families and individuals within your congregation. Church life today is often limited to weekly attendance, with very little interpersonal sharing beyond a casual, "Hi, how are you?" If you have a growing burden to care for the physical and material needs of others, you can encourage small-group ministries (Bible studies, prayer groups, family-support groups, care clusters, discipleship groups, and other fellowship-oriented small groups in which the group members get to know each other in-depth). These will provide everyone who attends your church with an opportunity to develop real caring relationships with other Christians.

Second, if your church members do reach out to minister within the non-Christian community (something every church ought to do), you will be more effective if your outreach is built upon an existing caring ministry among your own members. The experience you gain in your own church will also establish your credibility for a broader ministry in the community.

So don't assume that all is well spiritually or materially among your fellow members. Instead, work to provide small-group caring and shepherding ministries which will watch out for all of your church members' and attenders' spiritual and physical needs.

Begin where you are, then move out in ever-widening spheres of influence. Jesus' statement in Acts 1:8 suggests this key ministry principle: "Be my witnesses in Jerusalem, and in all Judea and Samaria, and to the ends of the earth." If your local church wants to minister effectively in the world beyond its walls, you must first model a life of caring *within* your fellowship. Demonstrating how God transforms self-centered lives into others-centered sharers should be every local church's priority. The Christian community must model an attractive, biblically-based, alternative life-style.

Begin where you are, with what you have, and do what you can. This principle summarizes all you need to begin a caring ministry. You don't need an office, a name, a staff or any resources beyond those you already have at your disposal. A growing vision of what God is calling you to do, His Word, regular times with Him in prayer, sensitivity to the Holy Spirit's leading, and one or two friends who share your concern is all you need to get started.

Form a Small Group for Study and Support

Personal study will help you share your vision with a small support group and give you useful information to use when recruiting a band of committed individuals who will share responsibility for carrying out your caring ministry. Many excellent resources are available for support groups who want to meet together regularly for guided discussions, to pray, to support one another, and to discuss specific applications within their local churches. Together you can plan a small group study that includes personal Bible study and some discussions on the needs of people within your local church and the local community.

Three of the most helpful books for small-group study and discussion are: Donald B. Kraybill's *The Upside Down Kingdom* (Herald Press, 1978), Ronald J. Sider's *Rich Christians in An Age of Hunger* (Inter-Varsity Press, 1977), and Tom Sine's *The Mustard Seed Conspiracy* (Word, Inc., 1981). You can read any of these books for personal study, but they can also provide a basis for group study and discussion. Inviting a few singles or couples to join you in a small study/discussion group which reads and discusses a chapter from one of these books every couple of weeks or so is one of the best ways to start your own caring/action ministry.

Some other more advanced but equally valuable resources include John Perkins' *With Justice for All* (Regal Books, 1982), Waldron Scott's *Bring Forth Justice* (Wm. B. Eerdmans Publishing Co., 1980), *Living More Simply*—Biblical Principles and Practical Models from the U.S. Consultation on Simple Lifestyle, edited by Ronald J. Sider (Inter-Varsity Press, 1980), and *Lifestyle in the Eighties*, also edited by Ronald J. Sider (The Westminster Press, 1982) which is a collection of papers presented at the International Consultation on Simple Lifestyle held in London, England, in 1981. A valuable Bible study aid is *Cry Justice*—the Bible speaks on Hunger and Poverty, again edited by Ronald J. Sider (Inter-Varsity Press, 1980). Each of these excellent books contains a bibliography or suggested references for further study.

Gather a Group of Like-Minded Individuals

As you share your interest in starting a small action/study group, others who have similar concerns will express an interest in joining your group. Pray that as a result of your studies, God will give you a small group of like-minded individuals who really want to do something about meeting needs in your local church. After you pray, invite a few individuals or couples you know (and who you think will be interested) to join you for a series of small-group studies. Share your dreams with one another and pray together regularly.

Discuss how you can begin your ministry in your church. According to the current needs in your fellowship, you can jointly plan how you are going to make the transition from being a small and private study group of concerned individuals into a ministry team with a recognizable identity and ministry in the life of your local church. Or, you may decide to remain a small, informal study/action group.

Above all, model a caring life-style in your relationships with one another. Take a genuine interest in each person's spiritual and personal development and growth. Encourage group members to follow their interests and exercise their spiritual gifts in service to others.

As well as spending time together in prayer, study, and discussion, do some work projects together (you might work together on home maintenance projects, for example). Working together like this gives you a chance to get to know the members of your small group better. On-the-job fellowship during a work project deepens your team's unity, and also gives you specific ways to build servant hearts and skills among your team members. Work projects can range from helping someone move, to replacing a defective water heater, doing yard work for an elderly person, or painting a sick person's home.

The more deeply you know one another's strengths and weaknesses, the more easily you will be able to identify who should take certain responsibilities in your ministry. Some will be adept at various organizational skills, others will have superb practical skills. Some will be people-oriented and able to inspire and recruit others to join your ministry. Others will be more suited to tasks which require lots of patience and stick-to-it-iveness. Remember, too, to have fun together. Your shared joy in the Lord will become one of your greatest resources when you begin more demanding, time-consuming projects which tax your spirit and your physical strength.

Stay Involved with Other Church Ministries

While you are studying and working together, make sure that each of your group members participates faithfully in the church's other ministries and services. You will be able to accomplish far more, in the long run, if you can integrate your team into the church's total life and work. Avoid becoming narrow specialists who only have time for one kind of ministry activity. Give your time, your effort, your ideas, your finances, and your people to other ministries.

Nancy, the chairperson of her church's social concerns committee, took an active part when her church visited every residence in its neighborhood. She was as active in her church's evangelistic outreach as she was in the church's social ministry. Because Nancy was personally involved in many of her church's ministries, she was a well-known and respected member of her congregation. Whenever Nancy asks people to support the social concerns committee, they respond because she supports their ministries personally.

Finding the proper balance between serving others and developing your own ministry comes with experience. Initially, you might meet once or twice monthly with your caring ministry team for Bible study, prayer, and discussion. That will still leave your team members with plenty of time to take part in some of the other church activities and ministries as well.

Encourage Many to Join Your Ministry

Anyone with a heart to serve can participate meaningfully in a caring ministry. I know two "senior saints" who have significant personal ministries. Dick coordinates a local church's prayer ministry, and Edith has a strong personal ministry among internationals, refugees, and other seniors. Although both Dick and Edith are in the so-called post-retirement years, both are investing their lives in service for the Lord. You may find many "retired" missionaries, pastors, and lay people who will be eager to join with you in your caring ministry.

So, if you are leading a caring ministry, or trying to begin one, don't exclude people. Rather, try to provide everyone who is interested with some constructive way to join in. You will soon discover there is no shortage of opportunities for genuine servants, so don't turn away anyone who shows a real interest in your ministry.

But it will be wise to limit your core leadership group or planning team to a smaller group of four to six individuals. This facilitates decision-making, and provides a broad enough range of opinions to keep your ministry on track. Select those with gifts in leading, organizing, administering, and decision-making. But try to balance the personalities of your core team also. Members of the planning team especially need strong interpersonal skills, so be sure that each team member is committed to the group and able to work well with all of the other members.

The precise amount of time you should spend studying and strategizing and getting your ministry launched will depend on your team and the kinds of needs you discover in your church. Some groups may spend a year or so as a small group before becoming a recognized, approved ministry of your local church. While becoming an "official" ministry will be a worthwhile goal for some groups, others will prefer to remain an informal, unpublicized service group within the local body. I recommend the goal of becoming an approved, integrated part of your local church's ministry since your team can make a greater impact if your church leaders support you, and your whole congregation becomes informed about what your group is doing. In some churches, some groups will be able to blend their caring ministry into the life of the local church right away.

Adjust your expectations, and your ministry plan, to suit your church and the availability of a group of like-minded individuals who work well together.

Do what you can, draw encouragement from small signs of progress, and build up other members of the body. Your group members will often be the ones to sense when the time has come to make the transition from an unofficial small group to an official church-related ministry. If you lead a caring ministry, listen closely to your team members' ideas about when to try new things.

As your ministry team's vision clarifies in the course of growing together, working together, and serving together, you will need to write out your ministry objectives.

Write Out the Purpose and Goals of Your Ministry

Writing out your statement of purpose and goals will enable you to communicate effectively with anyone who wants to become involved in your ministry and your church leaders. A brainstorming approach is one effective way to begin drafting such a statement of purpose and goals. By brainstorming together every one on your team can take an active part in the process of coming up with a rough draft of your purpose and goals. This encourages a sense of ownership among group members.

At this brainstorming stage you want as many ideas as possible, including wild and seemingly impossible or unrelated ideas. Start by considering questions such as: 1) What are some of the needs in our church and community? 2) Which problems are we already equipped to tackle? 3) What needs do we think God wants us to deal with? 4) What are other churches doing in these areas of need? 5) How can we cooperate with other churches in solving some of these problems? As suggestions and ideas start to flow, don't criticize. Instead, encourage creative thinking and dreaming.

After an hour or so of sharing as many ideas as possible, take a break and get ready to begin narrowing your focus. When you reconvene, look for related ideas and ways to combine the earlier statements. Slowly a pattern will emerge and you will be able to narrow down the focus of your ministry purpose and identify some of your most important goals. If a large group takes part in the initial brainstorming, you may ask a smaller planning group to refine the rough draft before your next meeting. Most groups will be able to agree on a general, accurate statement after two or three sessions dedicated to defining your ministry purpose and goals.

Here's an example my Sunday School class developed while studying Christian life-style together. After meeting together for thirteen weeks, the members of the class decided to form an action group within our local church. This is our initial statement of purpose:

> To serve both the leadership and the membership of our church in a ministry of social concern
>
> To research social needs within our church

family—members and attenders—with a special emphasis on biblical responsibilities such as caring for the poor, widows, and the elderly

To provide support—regular fellowship and encouragement—for group members and to regularly inform them of opportunities for service

To explore opportunities for ministering to needy people beyond our church in the community at large and to link this concern with our church's evangelistic outreach

To take action in selected projects when existing church ministries cannot handle them and which the action group decides to adopt, coordinate, or sponsor

To form a world concern group to provide the congregation with information about international needs including evangelism and development

To provide resource people and information to the church's Christian Education program to provide for the regular study and discussion of social concerns and ministries

To study the global context for mission and become better informed about such issues as poverty, wealth, international development, social justice, and missions from the Third World, so we can pray intelligently and cooperate effectively with our brothers and sisters in the Third World.

Invite Church Leaders to Give Input

Once you have developed a similar outline for your ministry, invite your pastor, and some other leaders (elders, deacons, Sunday School teachers) to review your draft and give their input. Try to discuss your plan with your pastor and other leaders in person also. Give them plenty of time to review your first draft, and schedule a convenient time when they can meet with your complete group. Listen carefully to your leaders' counsel and suggestions. Incorporate their ideas as you refine your group's statement of purpose.

Often a pastor or group of leaders will be delighted to learn that a concerned group of lay persons has come together to develop such a ministry. Many pastors and church leaders want to see caring ministries begin in their church, and they pray faithfully that God will raise up concerned individuals to lead and organize them. You may be an answer to your pastor's prayers, if your church does not already have a systematic way of dealing with physical and material needs.

After your church leaders learn about your plans and give their input, you will sense that your dream is becoming a reality! You will have a group of like-minded individuals who have studied the biblical basis for social concern. Your group has begun researching the needs within your congregation, and your church's leaders have given you their encouragement and endorsement.

One individual, one couple, one family, one small group can grow into a church-wide ministry in a few weeks, months, or years, according to their maturity and the needs in their congregation.

Today, some churches may need to organize such a ministry as rapidly as possible so they can respond to emergency needs created by current economic conditions. In those situations, therefore, a social ministry may be organized by a pastor or by a group of church leaders. When this must be done rapidly, care should be exercised to make sure that the leader or the group entrusted with the responsibility for this ministry are mature believers whose hearts are in people-oriented caring ministries. Ideally, these will be individuals already known for their compassion and dedication to serving others—people who are competent to lead, organize, and carry out a caring project or ministry.

Although some will object that such people are hard to find, I believe there's a vast untapped reservoir of spiritually-qualified lay persons in our churches who have the necessary vision, skill, and heart for such a ministry.

Whether a local church's caring ministry evolves gradually or is quickly organized, the ministry should include the following basic elements:

1. A qualified leader or team of leaders
2. A well-defined ministry purpose and goals
3. The approval and support of the church's leaders
4. A core planning group who organize and make decisions
5. A broad involvement of many local church members
6. A commitment to serve leaders, members, and attenders
7. A growing vision, based on biblical principles
8. A growing practice of biblical community among those involved
9. An ability to link social service with the church's evangelistic outreach.

The Biblical Model of a Caring Ministry

The model caring ministry, which still provides a challenging and inspiring description for everyone concerned with developing or leading such a ministry today, comes from the book of Acts. What made those first-century believers so effective in carrying the gospel throughout the world?

When we read Luke's account of the young church in action, we notice many reasons for their amazing effectiveness. They were certainly dedicated believers. They also listened eagerly to God's Word whenever the apostles taught them its deep truths. They were joyful, bold witnesses to their faith in Christ also. And they met often for prayer and worship. But far more important than any of these isolated activities was the combined impact of their common life, their life together, their shared community life. As a family of God's people they demonstrated the transforming power of God's love in ways that had never been seen on earth before. The first-century believers have much to teach twentieth-century disciples about caring, sharing, and serving. Two passages from Luke's history of the expansion of the Christian movement describe what can happen when members of a local church allow God to govern their relationships with one another:

They met constantly to hear the apostles teach, and to share the common life, to break bread, and to pray. A sense of awe was everywhere, and many marvels and signs were brought about through the apostles. All whose faith had drawn them together held everything in common: they would sell their property and possessions and make a general distribution as the need of each required. With one mind they kept up their daily attendance at the temple, and, breaking bread in private houses, shared their meals with unaffected joy, as they praised God and enjoyed the favour of the whole people. And day by day the Lord added to their number those whom he was saving . . . . The whole body of believers was united in heart and soul. Not a man of them claimed any of his possessions as his own, but everything was held in common, while the apostles bore witness with great power to the resurrection of the Lord Jesus. They were all held in high esteem; for they never had a needy person among them, because all who had property in land or houses sold it, brought the proceeds of the sale, and laid the money at the feet of the apostles; it was then distributed to any who stood in need (Acts 2:42-47; 4:32-35, *NEB*).

Reread this moving account of the joyful common life of the Jerusalem church, and ask God to give you a vision of how to encourage modern believers to live together in ways that will demonstrate God's love. Pray about how you can nurture an authentic, biblical style of community caring and sharing in your local church. Then do what God leads you to do.

Tom Sine observes that the church in the twentieth century can be renewed through a rediscovery of community. Like the Jerusalem church, we must spend ourselves, our time, talents, and finances in service to one another, and to the needy members of our society.

> Our goal then must be to strive as authentically as possible to incarnate the life and values of Jesus in our life together . . . . In the first community, Jesus and the Twelve modeled the values of the new future of God in every dimension of life. All their relationships, including their economic ones, were transformed by the inbreaking of God's future into their midst. They shared a common purse not only among themselves, but with their followers and the poor . . . . The reason believers were able to share in this extraordinary way was that their values had been profoundly changed by Christ; they no longer lived for themselves. Their lives were devoted to the service of God, his kingdom, and his world. Through their sharing, they not only modeled the new age of economic justice; they also freed up resources for the work of justice in their own day.[1]

Peter H. Davids, a New Testament scholar and an associate professor of Biblical Studies at Trinity Episcopal School for Ministry in Ambridge, Pennsylvania, notes that "Luke presents the descriptions of Acts not simply as local ideals, but also as descriptions of what to some extent all churches he knew were like."² Davids also comments helpfully on the Jerusalem Christians' extraordinary willingness to sell their property and give the proceeds to the apostles:

> It is sometimes wrongly assumed that the communal sharing . . . indicates a total rejection of private ownership. The text points to a somewhat different situation. There was certainly a subjective release from a need for private possession . . . But the objective divestiture and redistribution of goods in both passages was a process which took place gradually according to the needs of the community. Sharing was not a rule to be followed but a result of deep spirituality, of mutual love and care.³

Caring ministries, in which caring lay persons encourage believers to freely share their lives and their resources with one another in local churches, are needed now more than ever. Modern man will never be convinced of the truths of the gospel unless he sees real Christians living out the consequences of the new birth in practical ways. Local churches must care for the needy in our society, but if we are ever to accomplish that goal we must begin by caring for the needy within our local fellowships first.

In *The Cost of Discipleship* Dietrich Bonhoeffer stresses the need for practical brotherly living within the Body of Christ. He shows us how the practice of community should affect our interpersonal relationships with our brothers and sisters in Christ. If we can apply these insights within the local fellowship of believers, we can expect to see God use us as we express His love to the needy men and women and children in the world around us. Bonhoeffer writes:

If the world despises one of the brethren, the

Christian will love and serve him. If the world does him violence, the Christian will succour and comfort him. If the world dishonours and insults him, the Christian will sacrifice his honour to cover his brother's shame. Where the world exploits, he will dispossess himself, and where the world oppresses, he will stoop down and raise up the oppressed. If the world refuses justice, the Christian will pursue mercy, and if the world takes refuge in lies, he will open his mouth for the dumb, and bear testimony to the truth. For the sake of the brother, be he Jew or Greek, bond or free, strong or weak, noble or base, he will renounce all fellowship with the world. For the Christian serves the fellowship of the Body of Christ, and he cannot hide it from the world. He is called out of the world to follow Christ.[4]

Here is the contemporary challenge for all local churches. We must return to a more biblical life-style. We must become more accountable to and for one another in every area of life. The church exists to model the infinite, cross-cultural, trans-racial love of God. Our belief must affect our behavior. We must translate our theology into Christlike deeds of loving service. We can dare to believe that God will use us to change individual lives, churches, communities, and even nations world-wide—if we are individually willing to act out our devotion to Christ. Our world needs good Samaritan faith—faith that results in action. We need individuals who will purposefully develop caring life-styles and ministries. Will you help fill this need?

If you share this vision, begin where you are—in your local church—use the resources you already have, and do what *you* can.

For Study or Discussion

1. Think of three or four people you know in your church or neighborhood who might be interested in starting a "caring group." Write down their names. How could you approach them to explain how you feel about getting personally involved with others' needs? Write out reasons why you should all form a caring group.

2. Even though you may not yet have an organized group, read again the sample "statement of purpose" in this chapter and write a purpose and some goals for such a group.

3. Read again Acts 2:42-47 and 4:32-35 in your own Bible and pray that God will give *you* a vision of ways to demonstrate His love to those who are in need, whether spiritually or materially.

4. As you consider the needs and opportunities for caring within your local church, describe what you would like to see God accomplish in one of those areas during the next year.

5. Reread Luke 10:25-37. As you meditate on the parable of the Good Samaritan, pray that God will use you to demonstrate your faith by helping needy people in practical ways.

6. Think back over what you have learned while reading, studying, or discussing this book. Choose one specific way in which you can serve someone with a practical need, and commit yourself to a definite plan to do that within one to two weeks. Be a good Samaritan in your home, church, and community!

Notes
1. Tom Sine, *The Mustard Seed Conspiracy* (Waco, TX: Word Books, 1981), pp. 173,175.
2. Peter H. Davids, *Living More Simply* (Downers Grove, IL: Inter-Varsity Press, 1980), pp. 45-46.
3. Ibid., p. 46.
4. Dietrich Bonhoeffer, *The Cost of Discipleship*, (New York: Macmillan Publishing Company, 1978), pp. 289-290.

Bibliography

Aldrich, Joseph C. *Life-Style Evangelism.* (Portland, OR: Multnomah Press, 1981).

Bonhoeffer, Dietrich. *The Cost of Discipleship.* (New York: Macmillan Publishing, 1978).

Costas, Orlando E. *The Integrity of Mission* The Inner Life and Outreach of the Church. (San Francisco: Harper and Row Publishers, 1979).

Doig, Desmond. *Mother Teresa and Her Work.* (San Francisco: Harper and Row Publishers, 1976).

Douglas, J.D., ed. *Let the Earth Hear His Voice.* (Minneaplois, World Wide Publications, 1975).

Evangelical Concern of Denver. *How You Can Be a People Helper.* (Denver, 1983).

Henry, Carl F.H. *A Plea for Evangelical Demonstration.* (Grand Rapids: Baker Book House, 1971).

Johnstone, Patrick. *Operation World.* (Bromley, England: Send the Light Publications, 1978).

Jones, E. Stanley. *A Song of Ascents.* (Nashville: Abingdon Press, 1968).

Kraybill, Donald B. *The Upside Down Kingdom.* (Scottdale, PA: Herald Press, 1978).

Lausanne Occasional Papers No. 21—Grand Rapids

Report—*Evangelism and Social Responsibility* An Evangelical Commitment. (Lausanne Committee and the World Evangelical Fellowship, 1982).

Mott, Stephen. *Biblical Ethics and Social Change.* (New York: Oxford University Press, 1982).

O'Connor, Elizabeth, *The New Community.* (San Francisco: Harper and Row Publishers, 1976).

Pinson, William M. *Applying the Gospel* Suggestions for Christian Social Action in a Local Church. (Nashville: Broadman Press, 1975).

Perkins, John. *With Justice for All.* (Ventura, CA: Regal Books, 1982).

Peters, George. *A Theology of Church Growth.* (Grand Rapids: Zondervan Publishing House, 1981).

Petersen, Jim. *Evangelism as a Lifestyle.* (Colorado Springs: NavPress, 1981).

Rifkin, Jeremy, with Howard, Ted. *The Emerging Order* God in the Age of Scarcity. (New York: G.P. Putnam's Sons, 1979).

Schaeffer, Francis. *The Church at the End of the Twentieth Century.* (Downers Grove, IL: Inter-Varsity Press, 1970).

Scott, Waldron. *Bring Forth Justice* A Contemporary Perspective on Mission. (Grand Rapids: Wm. B. Eerdmans Publishing Co., 1980).

Sider, Ronald J., ed. *Cry Justice* The Bible Speaks on Hunger and Poverty. (Downers Grove, IL: Inter-Varsity Press, 1980).

Sider, Ronald J., ed. *Lifestyle in the Eighties.* (Philadelphia: The Westminster Press, 1982).

Sider, Ronald J. *Rich Christians in an Age of Hunger.* (Downers Grove, IL: Inter-Varsity Press, 1977).

Sider, Ronald J., ed. *Evangelicals and Development* Towards a Theology of Social Development, Contemporary Issues in Social Ethics, Volume 2. (Exeter, England: The Paternoster Press and the World Evangelical Fellowship, 1981).

Simon, Arthur. *Bread for the World.* (New York: Paulist

Press/Grand Rapids: Wm. B. Eerdmans Publishing Co., 1975).

Sine, Tom. *The Mustard Seed Conspiracy.* (Waco, TX: Word, Inc., 1981).

Snyder, Howard A. *Liberating the Church.* (Downers Grove, IL: Inter-Varsity Press, 1983).

Stott, John. *Christian Mission in the Modern World.* (Downers Grove, IL: Inter-Varsity Press, 1979).

Tillapaugh, Frank. *The Church Unleashed.* (Ventura, CA: Regal Books, 1982).

Wagner, C. Peter. *Church Growth and the Whole Gospel.* (San Francisco: Harper and Row Publishers, 1981).

Wallis, Jim. *Agenda for Biblical People* A new focus for developing a lifestyle of discipleship. (San Francisco: Harper and Row Publishers, 1976).

Warren, Roland L. *Studying Your Community.* (New York: The Free Press, 1965).

White, Jerry. *The Church and the Parachurch* An Uneasy Marriage. (Portland, OR: Multnomah Press, 1983).

White, John. *The Golden Cow* Materialism in the Twentieth Century Church. (Downers Grove, IL: Inter-Varsity Press, 1979).

Wirt, Sherwood Eliot. *The Social Conscience of the Evangelical.* (New York: Harper and Row Publishers, 1968).

Scripture Index

OTHER GOOD READING
FROM REGAL BOOKS

☐ **Measure of a Church,** Gene A. Getz—A study to help evaluate the vital signs of a church by comparing it to the growing churches of the New Testament. — $3.50 5014700

☐ **Love, Acceptance and Forgiveness,** Jerry Cook with Stanley C. Baldwin—Discover how your church can provide an atmosphere of love, acceptance and forgiveness as people minister to people. — $4.95 5411106

☐ **Body Life,** Ray C. Stedman—A study of the church as Christ's Body, each member's obligation to exercise his individual gifts, and the implications for church renewal. — $6.95 5413400

☐ **Your Spiritual Gifts Can Help Your Church Grow,** C. Peter Wagner—A thorough, practical look at spiritual gifts and how they can play a part in helping any church grow. — $7.95 5410606

☐ **Church Unleashed,** Frank R. Tillapaugh—Any church can grow by extending its ministry beyond its facilities and into the community. — $5.95 5416300

☐ **Lord, Make My Life a Miracle,** Raymond C. Ortlund—An account of spiritual growth when three major priorities of life were properly arranged. — $3.50 5011701

Buy these books at your local bookstore or use this handy coupon for ordering:

Regal Books, P.O. Box 3875, Ventura, CA 93006
Please send me the book(s) I have checked above. I am enclosing $_____.
(Orders under $20.00 add $1.00 shipping and handling, over $20.00 add 10%. All California orders must include 6% sales tax.) Send check or money order— no cash or C.O.D.

Please charge my ☐ VISA   Card # _____
                 ☐ MasterCard   Exp. Date _____

Name: _____

Address: _____

City: _____ State/Zip: _____

Please allow 2-4 weeks delivery. U.S. prices shown. Prices subject to change without notice.